Information Security Managen

Other publications by Van Haren Publishing

Van Haren Publishing (VHP) specializes in titles on Best Practices, methods and standards within four domains:
- IT management,
- Architecture (Enterprise and IT),
- Business management and
- Project management

VHP is also publisher on behalf of leading companies and institutions:
The Open Group, IPMA-NL, PMI-NL, CA, Getronics, Quint, ITSqc, LLC, The Sox Institute and ASL BiSL Foundation

Topics are (per domain):

IT (Service) Management / IT Governance
ASL
BiSL
CATS
CMMI
CoBiT
ISO 17799
ISO 27001
ISO 27002
ISO/IEC 20000
ISPL
IT Service CMM
ITIL® V2
ITIL® V3
ITSM
MOF
MSF
ABC of ICT

Architecture (Enterprise and IT)
Archimate®
GEA®
TOGAF™

Business Management
EFQM
ISA-95
ISO 9000
ISO 9001:2000
SixSigma
SOX
SqEME®
eSCM

Project/Programme/ Risk Management
A4-Projectmanagement
ICB / NCB
MINCE®
M_o_R®
MSP™
PMBOK® Guide
PRINCE2™

For the latest information on VHP publications, visit our website: www.vanharen.net.

Information Security Management with ITIL® Version 3

Jacques A. Cazemier,
Paul Overbeek,
Louk Peters

Van Haren PUBLISHING

Colophon

Title:	Information Security Management with ITIL® V3
Series:	Best Practice
Authors:	Jacques A. Cazemier, Paul Overbeek, Louk Peters
Editor:	Jane Chittenden
Publisher:	Van Haren Publishing, Zaltbommel, www.vanharen.net
ISBN:	978 90 8753 552 0
Print:	First edition, first impression, January 2010
Design and Layout:	CO2 Premedia, Amersfoort-NL
Copyright:	© Van Haren Publishing, 2010
Printer:	Wilco, Amersfoort – NL

For any further enquiries about Van Haren Publishing, please send an e-mail to: info@vanharen.net

Contents

About the authors

Ing. Jacques A. Cazemier is Management Consultant at Verdonck, Klooster & Associates (VKA), an independent consulting company in the Netherlands.

Dr. ir. Paul Overbeek RE is partner with OIS Information Risk & Security Management and lectures at the universities of Amsterdam, Rotterdam and Tilburg.

Drs. Louk Peters is senior business consultant for Getronics Consulting, one of the founding organizations for ITIL.

Acknowledgements

In theory, there is no difference between theory and practice. In practice there is.

This book has been written to show theory and practice of dealing with Information Security Management. We share our experiences of aiding organizations in incorporating information security management. Those experiences would not have been possible without the continuous contributions from people who – just like us – are dealing with information risks on a daily basis.

We would like to thank the reviewers who provided valuable comments on the texts we had written. In alphabetical order they are:
Dr Gary Hinson, IsecT Ltd
David Jones, Pink Elephant UK
David Lynas, SABSA Foundation
Paul Peursum, DNV-CIBIT, The Netherlands
Rita Pilon, EXIN International
Dr Gad J Selig, University of Bridgeport, USA
Dr Abbas Shahim, Atos Consulting, The Netherlands
Takanori Tsukada, Hitachi Software Engineering Co., Ltd., Japan
Xander van der Voort, vanderVoort Projects, The Netherlands

Executive summary

Challenges

In recent years there have been developments that require more confidence in information and information processing. Those developments range from regulations and directives to pressure from stakeholders and from changes in use of technology to increased liability.

As organizations have become increasingly dependent on electronic delivery of services, the importance of maintaining high standards for information technology (IT) performance is increased as well. Information is one of the most important assets for business; sharing of information with other organizations adds to that importance.

Information is also becoming more vulnerable: it can deteriorate, it may fall in the hands of an unauthorized person, it may be corrupted, and it might not be available when needed. It is increasingly threatened by deliberate attack and by unintentional security incidents such as the loss of huge numbers of personal records stored electronically.

In addition, legislation and regulations mandate governance and compliance. Information security provides the basis for these aspects: assurance that information is reliable and information processing is sound. Information has to be provided to prove compliance. Add to that the need to manage IT costs and it is clear that maintaining the required level of information security is a major challenge.

Solutions

For IT, information and the power to process this essential asset is the core of its existence. Endangering information or its processing will immediately threaten the business. For that reason, securing information as well as the IT that processes it is an important subject.

Just maintaining the required level of information security is not sufficient. It is essential to have continuous security improvement to the level where risks are still acceptable. This does not stop at building more technology to repel threats or strengthening procedures. It also means managing the required level of security.

This book provides the background to enable adequate information security. It is an update of ITIL® (IT Infrastructure Library) version 2 Security Management book [CAZ] and fits within the ITIL version 3 service lifecycle. It also makes reference to international standards like ISO/IEC 20000 and ISO/IEC 27001. ITIL® is a registered trademark of the UK Office of Government Commerce.

This book describes Information Security Management with ITIL version 3 and builds on the ITIL version 3 processes and activities that are required to manage IT effectively.

Results

The benefits of sufficiently secure information extend to the entire business, from corporate image and position in the market to effectiveness and efficiency. It provides inherent flexibility: because information and IT security is controlled, robustness and reliability are ensured. Demonstrable compliance and continuous adherence to regulations form the basis for all business processes that require use of information and information processing.

Information Security Management gives IT resilience to survive, whatever the storms that threaten the business.

X

1 Introduction

1.1 This book

Information security is one of the subjects with wide coverage on the Internet. Texts on improving security, as well as breaching security, are just a few clicks away. This phenomenon is one of the reasons that maintaining information security is such an important subject: ignorance of your own information security is an open invitation to serious problems in everything that your information is used for. Without continuous effort to maintain an adequate level of protection, all investments in reliable information processing will lose their value and processes dependent on trustworthy information will fail.

Information security is an essential requirement for organizations that use and rely upon information since information is a volatile corporate asset. Commonplace security risks to information assets include:

- fraudsters inside or outside your organization who exploit missing or weak process controls for personal advantage
- theft or unauthorized disclosure of proprietary or personal data (e.g. industrial espionage, inappropriate web publication)
- human errors and omissions by information users, system/network administrators and operators (e.g. inaccurate or incomplete data entry, mis-configuration of technical security controls)
- malware – malicious software such as network worms and Trojan horse programs
- hackers who deliberately attempt unauthorized access to systems
- technical vulnerabilities arising from programming errors and design flaws in computer software, firmware and hardware (bugs and so forth)
- physical damage or loss of IT equipment and information storage media arising from storms, floods, lightning, sabotage, accidents and thefts.

In the ITIL context, many of these risks are likely to affect the organization's provision of IT services unless suitable information security controls are in place. However, information security controls require resources to design, implement, manage and utilise, hence management needs to strike a balance based on the costs and benefits of security.

Management effort is required in order to maintain the required level of security. Since information security is not limited to one aspect of technology, personnel or process, management will need to have relationships with all processes in the organization. The consequence is that Information Security Management needs to be part of every process. In this book, Information Security Management is shown to be present in all phases of the lifecycle of ITIL version 3.

1.1.1 Context

This book is an update of the ITIL book Security Management, which is a title in the ITIL version 2 series. The reason for this update is twofold: it reflects the updates of ITIL version 3 and it adds new developments and changes to the previous version.

The update consists of:
* explaining the most important changes of ITIL version 3, as far as information security management is concerned
* incorporating the changes to Information Security Management as a result of updated standards and best practices
* describing new trends in information security and its management
* highlighting the increased importance of outsourcing and service orientation
* focusing on business aspects and practices.

In this book, Information Security Management is covered from setting the initial security objectives to implementation and maintenance. It shows the relationships to all processes and activities that interface with information.

Information Security Management is a management process. It is not restricted to information technology. It is not sufficient to limit information security management to computers, networks and software. Information on other media – like paper – will have to be protected as well. It is not restricted to people; and it is not restricted to processes. For example, countermeasures for threats to information security will be found in areas as diverse as organizational architecture, human resources, computer hardware and software, physical access to buildings and supply of electrical power.

Taking ITILv3 as the starting point also gives some limitations. The focus of Information Security Management in this context is more on information, IT and business alignment and less on topics that are also relevant for security including legal aspects, organizational change, HR management and facilities.

Target audience
This book is intended for IT managers and business managers who are looking for practical directions to maintain Information Security Management. It may also be useful to business process managers to understand what Information Security Management is about.

1.1.2 Best practice
The value of this book lies in its character as best practice. It integrates current standards and best practices. It is not a standard that would be used for a certification process, it is not a regulation to be followed to the letter. It provides ideas and experiences that may or may not be appropriate in your situation. We believe that the overall advice in this book is useful in the majority of cases; however, it may need to be adapted to your organization's situation.

The book enables comparison of experiences and informed discussions about implementation of Information Security Management. In addition, it may serve as a benchmark when organizations are comparing their efforts in this field.

1.1.3 The subject
Information security management is the process to ensure that both information and information processing is (and remains) reliable, confidential and available when and for whom it is required. It limits access to information and information processing to authorized people and functions.

Information Security Management deals with establishing and maintaining all that is needed to keep that required level of information security.

The basis for this required level is the specification of information security in the Service Level Agreement that has been agreed between the business and the service provider.

The goal of Information Security Management is to provide confidence and assurance to the business that the business assets are protected and the overall security process supports the business mission. Security has long been seen as a subject for the IT department, with much emphasis on technology. Solving business problems was never considered as a reason for security measures. Although the introduction of the standard BS7799 (later ISO/IEC 27002) made it clear that security is about more than technology alone, in practice we still see a silo approach towards security, so that security restricts business processes and even sometimes becomes a showstopper or restraint.

With a 'guard-dog' attitude, IT departments used to think that a secure IT infrastructure could only be established by just enforcing more rules, more and longer passwords, more limitations on access, more firewalls and the like. This approach has given security a bad reputation, sometimes called 'the business prevention department'.

Security is not an end in itself but a property relative to a specific (business) context. What is good for one organization does not necessarily have to apply to another. For others, there will be other risks. There is a definite need for 'tailored security'.

How to define and reach the required level of security – that is, how to determine which control objectives are needed and what controls are to be put in place to reach the required level of security – is one part of Information Security Management. It contains topics such as establishing the proper business requirement for information security, risk analysis, defining control objectives, the definition of the right countermeasures, creating a standard minimum level of information security, the implementation of controls and operational monitoring such as intrusion detection.

The other part of Information Security Management deals with maintaining information security at the required level and providing appropriate assurance. Security maintenance topics are incident registration and handling, trend analysis and reporting, escalation support, access management, hardening, maintaining standards, etc.

The first part, defining and reaching the required level of security, is performed first. When information security is 'in place', operational and functioning, the second part (maintaining the required level) is a continuous effort as part of the lifecycle. The activities are essentially the same as for the first part, but become progressively better informed by metrics and experience of the operational security management system. Of course, the requirements for security have to be maintained as well. These are not static since both the importance of information as well as the threats in the ever-changing IT and organizational infrastructure vary.

The Information Security Management process coordinates and directs the security activities, using a standard process management cycle.

This book's primary focus is the Information Security Management system, which resembles a normal management process like that of the ISO 9000 series of standards. This management system maintains the required level of security, reacts to problems and improves controls and countermeasures and security management itself if necessary.

Since Information Security Management has relationships with almost all other management processes and is part of many organizational activities, it is impossible to operate information security as a standalone process. The relationships to other processes and the management activities required to maintain an overview of information security are the main subjects of this book.

Managing information security has become a critical business issue. Compliance dictates demonstrable control and auditability, for which Information Security Management is mandatory. Proving that the organization is in control of its information security is high on every business's agenda – or should be.

1.1.4   Trends in information security

Information processing and the required technology are changing in ways that are increasingly rapid and complex. The Internet and its services have become part of our social and business structure. This creates challenges when implementing hardware and software infrastructure (and subsequent infrastructure), administration, management, maintenance and support. Keeping up to date with security adds to that burden. This paragraph sketches just a few of the many developments that affect information security today.

A particular challenge is created by the fact that every security flaw that is ever found is published on the Internet. Add to this the availability on the Internet of construction kits for all kinds of malicious programs to exploit these flaws. Keeping up with and responding rapidly to the continual flow of security bulletins, patches and updates are more essential than ever.

Fortunately, security awareness is improving and products are being designed with more security technology built in. Initiatives such as sourcing and Service Oriented Architectures are stimulating professionalism in service and system management and are promoting the use of tools to support Information Security Management.
Suppliers are providing more or less integrated security embedded in their management tools, which allows centralized monitoring and resolving of security aspects. Networks, databases and applications, access and asset classification management systems are increasingly integrated, leading towards enterprise wide IT management.

The world of digital communication, the Internet and doing business through networks is now part of our society. Unfortunately, the criminal world has discovered that substantial profits can be made by fraudulently manipulating business on the Internet. Identity theft is a new form of robbery. Cyber crime is rising. Pressure on information security countermeasures is increasing. This means that Information Security Management – to maintain the required level of security – is becoming ever more important.

In line with the increased focus on governance, control of information security is becoming much more important as a management issue. At the same time, the legal aspects of information security are receiving more attention. Management needs to be in control, and that has to be demonstrated; as a result, monitoring is being given more attention. Starting with monitoring the security operations, attention evolves towards Information Security Management monitoring. Performance 'dashboards' provide information on security status, tuned to the needs of different levels of management.

The world is evolving into an environment where all kinds of information systems are connected. Organizations operate in networks, which has an impact on information security. 'The chain is only as strong as the weakest link' is a very valid expression. In particular, the IT interfaces between organizations are well known as weak points. Too often, this is treated as a technological problem. The human aspect is vulnerable to social engineering [MIT] and adequate processes to manage the connections across these borders are known to be weak links. Indeed, Information Security Management across the borders of organizations will be the main challenge for many years to come.

Information systems are linked not only through professionally managed corporate networks, but also through 'user managed' or amateur home networks, private media centers, vending machines, etc. Technically, household appliances can be controlled using the Internet. This implies that information security has to be integrated in all those functions. The idea that information security is limited to fencing the company's owned infrastructure is obsolete. Information is accessible via an increasing number of channels, some controlled by the organization itself, some managed by a third party or even by the users itself. This is described by the Jericho Forum [JER] as the problem of de-perimeterization or perimeter erosion. The huge explosion in business collaboration and commerce on the Web means that today's traditional approaches to securing a network boundary are at best flawed, and at worst ineffective. Examples include:
• business transactions that tunnel through perimeters or bypass them altogether
• IT products that cross the boundary, encapsulating protocols within Web protocols
• security exploits that use email and Web to get through the perimeter.

Information security increasingly requires attention from more than just IT – not only technology, but also public and political acceptance of the use of technology.

Identity theft has increased dramatically over the last few years. This includes 'phishing' attacks, which are aimed at obtaining personal information for fraudulent activities (e.g. whose fictitious premise might lead to the closing of a given bank). Similarly, attacks may deploy other types of fraudulent activity with an economic impact, such as emails that promise easy access to funding for mortgages or refinancing. All types of organizations, profit or non-profit, have to deal with these new types of crime. Millions of Internet users have their identities stolen each year. The consequences of identity theft can be traumatic. For identity theft victims it may cost a great deal of money and many days repairing the damage to their good name and credit record. For organizations facing fraud it means direct and indirect financial loss or loss of public image. It also may mean that information stored in customer databases may become corrupted.

Identity management systems may be considered, but there are trade-offs. On the one hand, access rights and separation of duties are easier to manage centrally; on the other, it may increase vulnerability by having a centralized access point to identity information and processing.

Online and real-time auditing and vulnerability monitoring are now possible. Combined with upcoming techniques for monitoring and filtering, more effective Information Security Management is possible to a much greater extent than previously. Supporting standards, like ISO/IEC27004, help to provide more awareness of the status of information security.

Governments depend on technology to implement policies. For example, public sector organizations are using biometrics and radio frequency identification (RFID) tags in passports, centralized records and administration and chip cards for identification, payment, authentication procedures and storage of certificates. Unfortunately, there are many examples of too much haste during implementation, subsequently revealing the results of ad hoc solutions.

Long-term vision is required to achieve the right balance of the effects of timely implementation and incorporating lasting security. Transparency, the scope of use, access rights to the underlying system and democratic control are but a few of the aspects that will have to be considered. The requirements for information security have never been so important as now. Failure to integrate security could have major political impact.

There is also the explosion of malware variants, where malware consists of malicious software designed to infiltrate or damage a computer system: recent attacks include new strains of malware that consist of millions of distinct threats that propagate as a single, core piece of malware. This creates an unlimited number of unique malware instances.

As the number of available Web services increases and as a large number of browsers continue to support the unsafe use of scripting languages, we can expect the number of new Web-based threats to continue to increase.

We see an increase in activity from threats related to social networking sites. These threats have involved 'phishing' for username accounts or using social context as a way to increase the 'success rate' of an online threat. Spammers, sending unsolicited junk mail (spam) in selected European, Middle Eastern and African regions have been heavily promoting social networking sites. These threats will become increasingly important for IT organizations since staff often access these tools using corporate resources.

Virtualization technology will be incorporated into security solutions to provide an environment that is isolated and protected from the chaos of a general-purpose operating system environment. This technology will provide a safe environment for sensitive transactions such as banking and protect critical infrastructure such as the security components that protect the general purpose operating environment. However, virtualization is just as much a threat as a benefit to security. Hackers are actively employing mechanisms to subvert and compromise virtual environments.

Malicious attackers have changed their approach. Examples of social engineering attacks are almost too numerous to mention, but a few of the most popular are: fake codecs, instant messaging spreading malware (which appears to be from a known contact) contains a link to a malicious website or malicious file, malicious content on peer-to-peer networks (which claims to be a popular application, video, or music content, but is actually just malware) and so on.

With the Internet, users want services anytime, any place. With cloud computing we offer the ability to work on documents from almost anywhere. This is convenient, but also represents a potential risk to your security and privacy. If you, as a user, can access your documents and sensitive data from anywhere, then so can people with malicious or criminal intentions, if they can guess your password or find a security weakness in the Web-based application. The physical computers that these services reside on are also a very attractive target – if criminals can break into a computer room and steal some of the servers, they will potentially have access to thousands of people's information.

Last but not least, other emerging trends worth mentioning are:
- a growing focus on compliance, accountability, governance, demonstrable security, assurance and audit ability – the whole assurance question
- more emphasis on information rather than IT security
- more professional education of workers in the field through CISSP, CISA, CISM, SABSA, SANS, GIAC etc.
- designing the management of information security as a coherent, comprehensive and cost-effective management system, itself aligned if not integrated with other management systems (e.g. ISO/IEC 20000 and/or ITIL, ISO 9000 etc.)
- greater emphasis on physical, procedural, legal, compliance, policy and awareness controls etc. in addition to technical security controls
- organizations seek much more standardization and have a growing interest in certification.

1.1.5   Structure of this book
This book contains five major chapters; the annexes provide additional background information.

Chapter 2: Fundamentals of information security – to provide insight and give background about what is going to be managed. Topics such as types of security controls, business benefits and the perspectives of business, customers, partners, service providers, and auditors are covered.

Chapter 3: Fundamentals of management of information security – to explain what information security management is about and its objectives. Details are also given on implementing generic Information Security Management and the continuous effort required to maintain its quality.

Chapter 4: ITIL version 3 and Information Security Management – shows the links with the other ITIL processes. It builds on existing processes and activities as much as possible. By integrating the Information Security Management activities into existing processes and activities, the additional efforts are reduced as much as possible, keeping responsibilities where they should be. Effective Information Security Management is mainly achieved through coordination and allocation of activities within other processes.

Chapter 5: Guidelines for implementing Information Security Management – gives practical advice how to put Information Security Management into practice. From awareness in the organization via documentation required to maturity models; this chapter aims to describe best practices for realizing Information Security Management.

In the annexes of this book, more information is given about standards and other best practices. These standards all use different starting points but deal more or less with the same subject; this allows you to choose the right framework for your organization's needs.

1.1.6   Website

The websites www.itilv3ism.nl and www.vanharen.net provide additional background information on Information Security Management with ITIL v3. The websites are also available to provide feedback and share good practices.

2 Fundamentals of information security

This chapter describes information security from the perspective of the different stakeholders. These stakeholders include the business, customers, partners, regulatory parties, auditors and those responsible for oversight as well as the perspective of management of the IT infrastructure.

Information and information processing are crucial to support business processes. Nowadays IT not only supports the business but also acts as an enabler for generating new business (e.g. the opportunities offered by the Internet). Each organization has to deal with an ongoing stream of changes in the business and its environment, causing changes in security requirements as well. To manage these changing requirements, information risk and security management is an integral part of all business processes. With the right security, the business objectives are supported and their achievement is assured, even when internal or external negative influences occur or if the IT fails.

The growing dependency on information and IT (and rapid development of the supporting technology), necessitate a proper management of current and future security controls that reflect the ever-changing risks and security requirements. This management activity is referred to as Information Security Management.

The objective of Information Security Management is to align information security, including IT security, with the business requirements for security and ensure that information security is effectively managed in all service and Service Management activities. IT security is a subject within information security. IT security is targeted more towards all IT technical components, including application, servers, networks, firewalls, etc) whereas information security addresses the wider scope of the information itself.

2.1 Perspectives on information security

An organization has implicit and explicit objectives. Business processes take place in an organization in order to achieve these objectives. In executing these processes, the organization is increasingly dependent on a well-functioning information management; organizations are increasingly dependent on IT services to meet their business needs. In this context, information security is not a goal in itself but a means of achieving the business objectives. Figure 2.1 shows the different perspectives on information security.

How information management is organized depends on the type of organization and the nature of the products or services it delivers in support of its business processes. The organization collects data in order to make products or supply a service. The data is stored, processed and made available when it is needed. Those people concerned have to be able to rely on its integrity; and it is equally important to ensure that only those who are authorized to do so can gain access to this information. Confidentiality, integrity, and availability should be expected as normal conditions of business operations and should not be open to discussion. An organization must

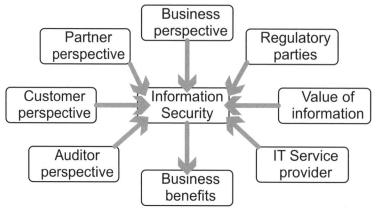

Figure 2.1: Different perspectives on information security

therefore organize the collection, storage, handling, processing and provision of information in such a way that these conditions are satisfied.

Information security exists to serve the interests of the business or organization; it is also relevant for other stakeholders with an interest in security – for example, individual data subjects or the authorities responsible for compliance obligations. Not all information and not all information services are equally important to the organization. The level of information security has to be appropriate to the importance of the information. This 'tailored security' is achieved by finding a balance between the security controls and their associated costs on the one hand and, on the other, the value of the information and the risks for the business in an information processing environment. Security in information systems can provide important added value. After all, having the right security for an information system means that more tasks can be performed in an accountable and responsible manner.

2.1.1 Value of information
Information security is intended to safeguard information. Security is the means of achieving an acceptable level of residual risks. Aspects that enable discussing the value of the information are:
* **confidentiality:** protecting sensitive information from unauthorized disclosure or intelligible interception
* **integrity:** safeguarding the accuracy, completeness and timeliness of information
* **availability:** ensuring that information and vital IT services are available when required.

Other aspects that are derived from the ones defined above include:
* **privacy:** the confidentiality and integrity of information traceable to a particular person
* **anonymity:** the confidentiality of a user's identity
* **authenticity:** the state in which there is no dispute about the identity of the participants involved
* **auditability:** the possibility of verifying that information is being used in line with the security policy and the ability of demonstrating that the security controls are working as intended.

The importance of having appropriate information management, and also adequate information security, is twofold for an organization.

Internal importance

An organization can only operate effectively if it has timely access to confidential, accurate and complete information. Information security has to be in line with this, ensuring that confidentiality, integrity and availability of information and information services is maintained.

External importance

An organization's processes supply products and/or services, which are made available in the market or the community, in order to achieve set objectives. Inadequate information security leads to imperfect products or services, thereby preventing the business objectives from being fully achieved and threatening the continued existence of the organization. Having adequate information security is an important precondition for adequate information management. Note that this applies to both the public and private sectors.

Besides the flow of results (products and services), countless information streams also flow from the external environment into the organization, internally through the organization, and from the organization out to the external environment. If these information streams suddenly dry up, the organization is no longer capable of operating effectively.

The requirements for adequate information security management reflect the degree to which the business processes depend on information. Information Security Management should form an integral part of an organization's overall quality management and quality assurance procedures as executed within the business processes. Therefore the requirements set for Information Security Management should largely come from the people who manage the business processes.

2.1.2   Types of security measures – controls

An important issue in Information Security Management is the degree to which an organization's management is able and willing to make a specific commitment to protecting the information, by making resources available: people, time and money. This commitment should be made on the basis of the available resources and the required level of information security, proportionate to the value of the information that has to be protected. Security measures can reduce the risks and vulnerability; they are also referred to as 'controls'.

Security measures make it possible to reduce or eliminate the risks associated with information and IT. The starting point, and by far the most important, is to have a good security organization, with clear responsibilities and tasks, guidelines, reporting procedures and measures that are appropriately matched to the needs of the business and the IT. Physical security measures, such as the physical separation of the data center, control physical access and provide a stable environment. Technical security measures provide security in an information system, operating system or network. This is, for example, the security offered by the operating system for the segregation of users. Process or procedural security measures describe how the staff is required to act in particular cases. For example, there must be procedures that describe who has access rights to the data center and when, or procedures that describe when a user's 'account' expires and what has to be done with the user's information after expiry of the account.

Security measures are effective only when used harmoniously with business processes. The security organization has to manage and maintain an appropriate balance.

Security measures can be used at a specific stage in the prevention and handling of security incidents, see figure 2.2. Security incidents are not predominantly caused by technical threats – statistics show that the large majority stem from human failure (intended or not) or procedural errors, and often have implications in other fields such as safety, legal aspects or health.

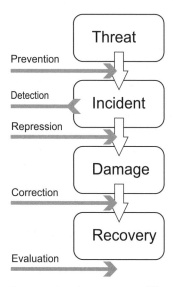

Figure 2.2: From threat to recovery; different types of countermeasures

The following stages can be identified. At the start there is a risk that a threat will materialize. A threat can be anything that would disrupt the business process or have a negative impact on business results. When a threat materializes, this is referred to as a security incident. This security incident may result in damage (to information or to other assets) that has to be repaired or otherwise corrected.

Suitable measures can be selected for each of these stages. The choice of measures will depend on the value of the information – that is, its importance to the business.
Preventive security measures are used to prevent a security incident from occurring. The best-known example of a preventive measure is the allocation of access rights to a limited group of authorized people. Further requirements associated with this measure include the management of access rights (granting, maintenance and withdrawal of rights), authorization (identifying who is allowed to access to which information and using which tools), identification and authentication (confirming who is seeking access), access control (ensuring that only authorized personnel can gain access).

If a security incident occurs, it is important to discover it as soon as possible: detection. A familiar example is monitoring, linked to an Event Management procedure. Another example is virus-checking software.

Repressive measures are then used to counteract any continuation or repetition of the security incident. For example, an account or network address is temporarily blocked after several failed attempts to log on or a bankcard is retained when multiple identification attempts are made with a wrong PIN number.

The damage is repaired as far as possible, using corrective measures. For example, corrective measures include restoring the backup, or returning to a previous stable situation (roll back, back out). Fallback can also been seen as a corrective measure.

In the case of serious security incidents, an evaluation is necessary in due course, to determine what went wrong, what caused the incident and how it can be prevented in the future. However, this process should not be limited to serious security incidents. All (near) breaches of security need to be studied in order to gain a full picture of the effectiveness of the security measures as a whole. A reporting procedure for security incidents and weaknesses is required to be able to evaluate the effectiveness and efficiency of the present security measures based on an insight into all security incidents and vulnerabilities. This is facilitated by the maintenance of log files and audit files, and of course, the records of the Service Desk function, which are discussed later in more detail.

2.1.3   The business perspective: how to manage information security

The starting point is effective organization of information security, in which responsibilities, authorities and duties are clearly specified in increasing levels of detail:

- policy and/or codes of conduct (**which control objectives** aligned with business requirements are we aiming for)
- processes (**what** has to happen to achieve those objectives)
- procedures (**who** does what and **when**)
- work instructions (**how** do we specifically do that, when and where and how does reporting take place).

Maintaining information security is a continuous process. All the factors that influence its results, and therefore have to be acted upon, are seen as inputs. There are internal and external influences that have their effect on information security. The internal influences stem from decisions within the organization. External influences come from the environment in which the business processes take place. This diversity makes Information Security Management a challenge.

Examples of changes in input which require adaptation of the process are:

- changes in business demands
- organizational changes, mergers, acquisitions
- changes in tasks or the importance of tasks
- physical alterations, e.g. after relocating business premises
- environmental alterations
- changes in assessment of the IT used
- changes in legislation
- changes in hardware and/or software
- changes in threats
- the introduction of new technology
- ageing or obsolete technology.

The result should be that, seen from a business perspective, the Information Security Management process provides a large degree of confidence that a certain level of confidentiality, integrity and availability has been achieved, that is sufficient for the business's purposes, and sufficient for the organization's (business) partners.

The developments in information security began in the early 1970s and took place independently of developments in IT management. Today, it is generally recognized that IT management and security are inseparable. The model below shows the management model for information security, from a business's perspective (figure 2.3).

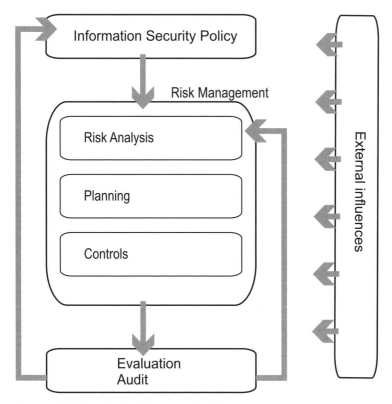

Figure 2.3: The Information Security Management System

The management system in figure 2.3 represents the complete information security process during all the phases of its cycle, from policy to maintenance. It is comparable to the management systems found in standards such as ISO 9000 and ISO/IEC 27001.

New business processes, at the earliest phase of formation, need to take information risks into account when considering business risks. This is also valid for existing business processes for which information security has never been an issue.

To determine what information security requirements are applicable and what countermeasures/ controls are required, a risk analysis is performed. The Information Security Management system consists of the closed loop created by evaluation and feedback to risk management of the process.

The risk analysis produces the details of the business case that supports investments in security. In this analysis, the requirements for security and details about risks become available; this information is used to detail information security in the security section of the Service Level Agreement (SLA), usually in the form of control objectives or a list of controls or countermeasures.

Information Security Management does not cover the details of performing such a risk analysis. For more details on the context of risk analyses within risk management, see ISO/IEC 27005.

In most organizations, information security and its management is governed by an Information Security Policy, whether as a separate document or as part of a larger (e.g. security or information) policy. With such a policy, consistency and coherence of processes and controls in the organization is dictated.

ISO/IEC 27005 is primarily concerned with risk analysis, the stage leading into the selection of security controls. ISO/IEC 27001 and ISO/IEC 27002 and ISO/IEC 27003 are more explicit on the planning, implementation and operation of security controls. The corporate information security policy provides direction to Information Security Management. It contains the mandatory management guidelines on, among other things, the organization, establishing the management control framework, responsibilities, scope and depth. This corporate policy is known under many names. It is sometimes part of (or related to) the Enterprise Risk Management policy, and policies for governance, risk, compliance or assurance.

Risk analyses should be performed to define the security objectives from a business perspective as well as from a technical perspective. These analyses make clear the current status and quality of information security (the current situation) as well as the security measures that are to be implemented (the desired situation). The required situation is described in a security plan or security handbook.

Planning is required to move from the current to the desired situation. After implementation, operation of the measures forms part of normal day-to-day operations. Management uses the management control framework to review the effectiveness and efficiency of the implementation of the security measures. These reviews also provide the necessary feedback to either improve the implementation or improve the plan. This input is used in the periodic (annual) security improvement plans, also known as risk treatment plan. The results of the audits also provide input to adapt the policy, or to improve the 'toolkit' for Information Security Management, including, for example, the risk analysis tools.

This book does not prescribe any risk analysis technique, such as ISO/IEC 27005 (Risk Management), IRAM (Information Risk Assessment Method from ISF) or the CCTA Risk Analysis and Management Methodology (CRAMM). Although risk analysis is required in identifying risks and the selection of measures, it should only be applied using a methodology that fits the organization and used where and when needed. Risk management and the selection of an approach that fits the objectives and maturity of the business are described later.

Management in general is concerned about money, as in cost and revenue. In information security measures, these aspects are to be treated seriously in order to avoid the perception of cost-only activity, so the outcome of a risk analysis should take the form of a balance, in which both risks and measures are (at least qualitatively) balanced between their 'costs' and their 'revenues'.

When a risk assessment is carried out professionally, management will obtain a positive view on information security and should be able to make decisions at the management level without the need to understand technical details.

2.1.4   A manager should be in control

Information security is about assurance. A manager should be 'in control'. Effective information security assures the continuity of the business, and the achievement of business goals.

To secure the IT infrastructure costs money (in terms of the cost of resources, maintenance and control). Not to secure the IT infrastructure also costs money (in terms of loss of revenues, costs of lost production, replacement costs of stolen or damaged data/equipment, compensation payments for unfulfilled contractual obligations). Estimating the costs requires business knowledge in order to produce meaningful financial values. It is even more important to estimate losses because of reputational damage, adverse publicity and loss of customer confidence. Reputational damage is not easy to quantify in financial loss. The financial aspects of Information Security Management are covered in section 4.1.4.

Effective Information Security Management depends on accurate risk analysis so that knowledge of the impact of risks and the costs of avoidance is understood. Without it, the tendency is either to ignore risks in the hope that they never happen, or spend disproportionate amounts of time and money on avoiding risks of minor potential impact. Risks are an inevitable feature of business life, and must be managed. Known risks, as well as unknown risks have to be managed: be prepared for the unexpected. Information Security Management is concerned with those activities that are required to maintain risks at manageable proportions, such as evaluation of effectiveness of measures, registration and trend analysis of security incidents.

2.1.5   Customer perspective

IT service providers have evolved into highly professional organizations. Customers of these service providers depend on their services to a large extend. In such a relationship, the professionalism of customer and service provider should be comparable, to enable a balanced relationship.

Figure 2.4: Trend in assurance and compliance

In the past, customers simply had to trust a service provider. Nowadays, under the pressure of legislation and regulations, customers require assurance about the security performance of their service providers that is based on evidence.

The movement from 'trust me' to 'prove to me' is a recent development (see figure 2.4). In Eastern cultures the focus has always been on trust, while in the Western world evidence has been more important.

In the process of specifying the Service Level Agreement (SLA), the service provider needs to ensure that it captures the customer's specified security requirements. If these requirements are matched with the security services from the service provider's Service Catalog, this is a benefit. The service provider can standardize its operation, which is easier to enforce and with less potential for error. It should also be more cost effective, since the same way of working is applied for more customers.

If the standard Service Catalog does not provide the required standard security services, then security services are tailored to the customer's need. This may be done via the Service Design phase of the service lifecycle.

Service providers can anticipate the need for confirmed assurance. The options below give some suggestions on how to provide sufficient assurance for groups of customers:
- **management assertion:** declaration of a service provider's management that a defined Information Security Management process is established and/or a certain internal or external standard is met
- **certification:** confirmation of a management assertion by a certification body, that an external standard such as ISO/IEC 27001 is met. The Code of Practice for Information Security Management (ISO/IEC 27002), provides best practices that help the organization to meet the requirements. Certification aims to address the requirements of a wide range of customers
- **third party conformation** by an independent auditor to report on the status of control objectives and controls of service organizations for use by user organizations and their auditors.

In addition to the required security services that are laid down in the SLA, a process (or at least a communication mechanism) should be established between the customer and the service provider to address security issues, including:
- common processes: incident management, authorization management, business continuity planning
- points of contact/responsibilities for the above processes
- reporting
- escalation mechanisms.

The security paragraph of the SLA is not limited to a description of control objectives. It should also define requirements for common processes, not only for maintaining objectives, but also for management of incidents, authorization and continuity. The SLA can, for example, address requirements for a common risk management process.

This alignment should be organized as part of the normal customer-service provider relationship model. Experience shows, however, that over time specific contacts for security issues emerge.

2.1.6 Partner perspective
More and more, parties are part of a value chain or network in which each link or node adds value to a service or product. An example is the distribution and supply chain, taking care of

physical goods. For each and every link in the chain, it is important that the quality of the information in the chain is known, and that it is timely. In value chains, two concepts for information management are commonly used:

- **centralized:** parties share information in a common place, that is managed by one of the participants or a service provider
- **decentralized:** parties distribute the information themselves across the relevant links in the chain.

Centralized information management
When parties share information in a common place, the requirements of all the participants should be analyzed and shared with the service provider. The situation is not very different from a 'customer'-'service provider' relationship as described above. Assurance can be organized in the same way.

Decentralized information management
Requirements should be communicated between the links. Because the links depend on each other, it is not sufficient to only address the needs of adjacent links; assurance must be organized over the whole chain.

Since in both models more parties are involved, standardization becomes even more important. For assurance, a common governance model, or a way to demonstrate compliance, has to be agreed upon. Accredited certification is valuable as a means for the organization to prove the existence of a standards-compliant information security management system without the need for each party in the chain or network to check security for themselves. There is a cost saving plus the adoption of generally accepted good security practices.

2.1.7 Oversight and auditing perspective
In today's governmental and business environment, 'assurance' is an ever-growing issue. An informal definition of assurance is: a level of certainty that something (a product, service or more generic organization behavior) meets defined criteria. These defined metrics usually imply compliance to agreed specifications, a norm or standard. 'Compliance' in broad terms, takes into consideration factors such as:

- the set of control objectives or controls that is to be implemented
- supervision, internal management oversight (e.g. using exception reports to identify situations that may deserve closer scrutiny; and internal auditing)
- review mechanisms (internal and external independent reviews, certification)
- awareness, training and educational activities to drive up compliance through understanding and appreciation of the requirements, pragmatic guidance and motivation
- sanctions, and the threat of sanctions
- the scope and quality of the standard or requirement against which compliance is sought (e.g. the Payment Card Industry Data Security Standard (PCI DSS)).

Compliance is often focused on external requirements, e.g. from legislation, the oversight body or customers. In that case compliance does not say much about the organization's own requirements for security.

When failure of one organization may have a high impact on all similar organizations in the same business segment, or on a group of consumers, assurance can be organized for this whole business segment by means of 'oversight'. In the banking and insurance environment, for example, oversight is there to stimulate and assure that all parties meet the assurance objectives set by the oversight body.

Oversight bodies have to balance their demands carefully. One the one hand, a dynamic commercial environment, aiming at innovation, competition and taking acceptable commercial risks, is to be stimulated and the cost of compliance should fit the purpose. On the other hand, the interests of all parties require that each of these parties acts responsibly, maintains a clear view on risks and limits these risks in such a way that continuity and stability can be expected. Two approaches, the rule-based and the objective-based, are used. In the rule-based approach oversight bodies present a detailed checklist with controls that are to be implemented. In the objective based approach oversight bodies set the objectives and the overseen entities have to explain their control selection that meets these objectives. In both cases, organizations have to demonstrate that controls have indeed been effectively implemented.

In short, IT auditors review risks relating to IT systems and processes including:
• inadequate information security
• inefficient controls, use of corporate resources or poor governance
• ineffective IT strategies, policies, controls and practices.

As part of their role, IT auditors check for compliance or conformance to agreed internal or external standards. Their requirement is that either their customer has a defined internal control framework, a set of control objectives/controls, or that an external standard can be adopted. Where processes are in place that provide for compliance, the auditor merely verifies that these processes are indeed adequate and perhaps validates a suitable sample. If these processes are defective or not present at all, the IT auditor has to gather evidence much deeper in the organization and the systems. This usually has a greater burden on the organization. For efficient auditing, the standards with which to comply should be defined beforehand, and the compliance processes, possibly supported by tools, should be implemented as well.

2.1.8 Perspective of the IT service provider

The IT service provider acts on identified customer requirements and has a security baseline (see 4.1.3 for an explanation of the concept) for its own security. Expectations of its customers about the quality of security services and evidence of their quality tend to grow rapidly. For an IT service provider communication about what is, and is not, part of the standard offering is important – not only for the purpose of managing the expectations of the customer, but also for legal reasons. If the limitations of the service offerings are not defined, the customer may reasonably expect their service to meet a level that is common in the market.

The definition of the security services can be part of the Service Catalog. Elements are: the Information Security Management process, a baseline for security control objectives, and reporting and sign-off. In addition the service provider offers security services in this Service Catalog, on top of the standard elements, on a commercial basis.

2.2   Security architectures

One of the definitions of 'architecture' used in ITIL (Service Design) is: 'the structure of a system or IT service, including the relationships of components to each other and to the environment they are in. Architecture also includes the standards and guidelines which guide the design and evolution of the system.'

This definition of 'architecture' comprises the design principles for:
• the objects themselves
• their relationships
• their interaction with their environment.

For example:
• an information system including hardware, software and applications
• a management system, including multiple processes that are planned and managed together, such as a Quality Management System
• a database management system or operating system that includes many software modules that are designed to perform a set of related functions.

Security architecture is defined along the same lines: a related set of entities that work together to achieve an overall security objective. 'Achievement' in security has two facets:
• the utility or functional aspect that a certain security functionality is offered, which makes the entity **fit for purpose** in establishing a secure environment
• the warranty or non-functional aspect of an entity that security is otherwise not compromised and cannot be bypassed, which makes it **fit for use** in a secure environment.

2.2.1   Security architecture relationships
Figure 2.5 shows the positioning of security architecture in the security framework.

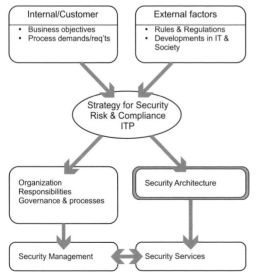

Figure 2.5: Security architecture relationship

The strategy for security, risk and compliance - see section 4.1 'Service Strategy' - is positioned in the center.

Architecture follows strategy. The strategy gives the boundaries of what can be done centrally and what is a local responsibility. The information security policy translates the business objectives, with support of risk assessment, into control objectives. These control objectives are realized through a set of controls that can be embedded in processes, be part of the culture of IT professionals, or are implemented in the domain of information and IT. The architecture needed for the latter part is a consequence of the choices reflected in the policy.

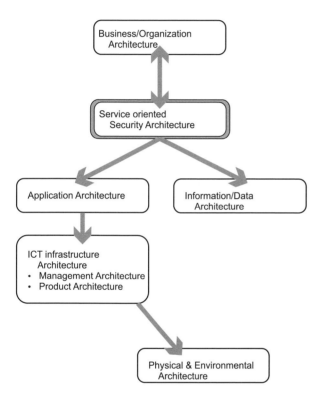

Figure 2.6: ITIL hierarchy of architectures

2.2.2 Elements of security architecture

The security architecture defines which *security services* are offered to whom. It also describes generic security guiding principles and security patterns to be used in designing new solutions not yet defined as services. The security architecture also provides *design guidelines* for new or renewed services. These two basic elements of security architectures are described below. In ITIL, a hierarchy of architectures is used. Figure 2.6 shows this hierarchy. The services of the security architecture are translated into protection:

• at the information/data level
• in the application

- in the supporting general infrastructure (platforms, networks, operating systems, generic applications, middleware, etc)
- in the wider environment, including cultural and physical aspects.

Note that a security service includes both the utility, the functional part, e.g. access control, as well as the warranty, the non-functional compliance part so that the functional part cannot be bypassed. The latter part, referred to as hardening, is not to be forgotten. Where the functional part may be offered somewhere in the hierarchy of functions, the compliance is required everywhere: a leakage of information at any place or level may jeopardize all good intentions in other places. However, the assumptions about what protection is expected where, as a precondition for effective behavior of a security service, must be made explicit. These 'conditions for effective usage' should be a standard part of each security product.

Other elements of the definition of a security service include:
- assurance, trustworthiness and proof of the reliability, suitability and quality of the service
- associated management activities and controls e.g. metrics, roles and responsibilities and accountabilities.

The security architecture defines the security services and the generic rules for implementation. Services can be centralized or decentralized, can be offered in the sub-architectures addressing information/data, application, infrastructure and environment, and can be implemented through a wide range of technical solutions. 'Identification and authentication', for example, can be a centralized or decentralized service. The challenge is to provide flexibility over time.

Examples of recognized practices for security architectures include:
- Enterprise Information Security Architecture
- Common Data Security Architecture/Open Group
- ISO OSI Security Architecture (enriched ISO 7498-2)
- Jericho Architecture and COA Framework (Jericho Forum/Togaf)
- RFC 4301: Security Architecture for the Internet Protocol
- ISO/IEC 10201: Security in the health environment
- NIST SP 800 series
- ISO/IEC 18028 -2: Network Security Architecture
- Octave
- SABSA

2.2.3 Common design principles for security services

The architecture gives the common design principles for security services. Given the speed of change, a first recommendation is to allow for evolution in the service and recognize the need for growth paths in the service offering itself. A challenge is to facilitate the ever-changing boundaries of protection, known as pre-, de- and re-perimeterization (see [JER]). It is normal that a security architecture evolves and that different concepts for protection co-exist for a longer period of time, which can be problematic.

The security architecture should provide design principles for security services. Key characteristics of the definition of a security service include:

- **functionality:** the service definition
- **trust models:** assumptions about the (unbroken and continuous) trustworthiness of the service itself and its environment
- **condition for effective use:** prerequisites, dependencies and possible interaction:
  - **boundaries:** is the service limited to a certain domain?
  - **trusted sources:** are these required and, if so, how are these identified and authenticated?
  - **environmental awareness:** is the service able to gain any required information about its environment?
  - **interaction:** if the service requires input or communication with other services, how is this interaction established?
  - **trust assumptions:** what protection is assumed from underlying layers, from other services, etc.? Is there a trustworthy part of the infrastructure? What is to be regarded as hostile or friendly?
  - **secure sessions:** is it possible to set up secure communication and, if so, which protocols are supported and how is identification, authentication, authorization and access control established?
- **management of the security service:**
  - central, decentralized, reporting, logging, monitoring, alerting
  - roles and responsibilities
  - ownership, responsibility, delegation
  - management of trust
- **resilience:**
  - hardening
  - vulnerability management
  - self-repair, fail safe defaults
  - survivability
  - 'graceful' degradation and revival
- **performance and capacity management**
  - recovery and contingency planning.

One of the challenges today is that some parts of the information, services and infrastructure are under the business's control and management, some may be outsourced under reliable security agreements, some may depend on partners in a chain of trust and some parts may be completely unknown.

2.2.4 Design principles for secure environments

Design principles for secure environments have evolved since 1975 [Sal]. They provide design principles that every architect, designer and developer in security should take into account.

- **isolation:** isolate critical components, monitor their behavior and keep them as simple as possible to enable controllability and auditability. Examples: firewall, centralized authoritative sources, cryptographic functions, etc.
- **fail-safe defaults:** deny everything that is not explicitly authorized. Reasons: create a fail-safe mode by preventing vulnerabilities caused by omissions or neglect. Examples: No access unless authorized, 'stripping' the web server operating system
- **complete mediation:** every access must be mediated. Reason: completeness. Examples: all external access must pass a firewall, all logins must pass the access control system, no back doors in the network, binding of functions so that these cannot be easily by-passed

- **open design:** security must not depend on secret design. Reasons: open design will be tested extensively and a secret design cannot be kept secret anyway. Examples: use well-known cryptographic algorithms, use proven technology, avoid home-made or end-user software
- **privileges: specify and separate.** Be clear about responsibilities and accountability. Be clear on reporting. Divide sensitive functions between different employees and/or services. Reason: create opposing interests, enabling the detection of fraud or error, and provide social barriers for fraud or abuse. Examples: separate granting of access from operational responsibilities, separate development from production, be specific on responsibilities for application management versus IT management, create a position for assigning user identities
- **limited functionality or least privilege:** components and users can only do what is necessary, so a functional need should exist ('need to use', 'need to access'). A more informal version is the 'need to withhold'. Reason: limit risk by cutting off potential vulnerabilities. Examples: menus based on authorizations, use protocols with defined limited functions, access only granted to identified and authorized components, limited access to operating system functionality, operational management through scripts only, run privileged functions under non-interactive limited accounts
- **compartments (levels, zones):** create separation so that activities from one compartment to another can be controlled and problems from one area cannot emerge/cross over to another. Reason: limit potential problems to a known specified area ('untrusted zone', e.g. the outside world) or concentrate security services on a known critical application area ('trusted area'). Examples: sub networks or zoning, Demilitarized Zone (DMZ)
- **ergonomics:** the interface must minimize the possibility of error and allow for error detection/correction. Examples: Rm –rf .*/*, 'to cancel, abort; press 'no' to continue'. Reason: prevent accidental error
- **redundancy:** never rely on a single barrier. Reason: be safe. Examples: access control both on application and operating system level, redundancy in web hosting, different paths to same destination, Raid-grade storage (Raid: 'redundant arrays of independent disk', today used to indicate the reliability of storage)
- **diversity:** never rely on multiple identical barriers. Reason: if one barrier is broken, everything is broken. Examples: two factor authentication, firewalls from different manufacturers, proxy and router
- **adaptability:** provide flexibility such that security mechanisms can be replaced over time. Reason: even the best security today may be insufficient or may be broken tomorrow. Examples: start with password security today, enable to add chip card tomorrow, and perhaps biometric techniques in the future; start with a cryptographic algorithm today but make sure it can be upgraded when required
- **resilience and survivability:** design services such that poor functioning is detected and recovered from. Enable the detection of vulnerabilities and controlled upgrades, fixing/automated patching. Define recovery points and safe states in case of failure. Reason: things will go wrong. Examples: 'hot fixing' newly detected vulnerabilities in operating systems, recovery points for databases
- **manageability:** make sure the service can be maintained and controlled
- **report:** a service must provide information on its own functioning and of defined events. Reason: enables manageability and detection of unwanted events. Examples: function reports, audit files, incident and event reporting, alarm messages.

Be aware that the boundaries are ever moving. In the last few decades many of the controls were bound to a specific geographical location with controls focusing on isolation of this environment with its local area networks and operating systems/platforms residing on hosts physically placed on that same location. Later on, an additional boundary of protection was added in the application layer. And now we see that since both data and applications become moving objects (sometimes with unknown or virtual locations), the controls are tied to the object of protection itself ('self defence'). An example of the latter is 'Jericho', the security architecture proposed by the Jericho Forum, part of the Open Group [JER]. All these developments will have to co-exist somehow. This is why it is important that services have an awareness of their operating environment so that events or incidents are more easy to recognise and can be anticipated upon, e.g. through limitation of their normal functioning.

The design of an architecture should not be an isolated exercise. From the start of the architectural design, it must be clear which common management processes (see figure 2.5 and 2.6) are required. This should ensure that the architecture and the management framework go together.

2.2.5 Common security services
The main common security services are:
- **identification:** recognizing an object (digital representation of a human being; application; network; machine; intelligent components, etc.)
- **authentication:** validation and accepting/rejecting of an assumed or declared identity. Often different levels of trust are supported for different purposes
- **authorization:** allowing/enforcing rights for access or execution of activities. Authorizations are often linked to objects. Many authorization mechanisms and methods exist. Examples are single use authorization; distributed, central or federated authorizations, etc. Authorization models may also address domains, roles, time-dependency, assurance and required evidence. Little standardization is available at present
- **access control:** enabling and enforcing access to information and/or activities limited to authorized objects only
- **boundary protection services:** geographical or logical boundaries are created, e.g. in networks to separate the trusted inside from the hostile outside world
- **secure communication services:** span the transfer between one safe domain, crossing untrusted domains, possibly to another safe domain
- **alarm, alerting, logging, monitoring:** signalling of defined events. Examples include monitoring of events, incidents, vulnerabilities and their follow-up, policy enforcement, etc
- **continuity services:** react to events that indicate that availability (such as response time) can be an issue or data loss is signalled to exceed a certain threshold. Example reactions include: enable the use of additional resources; gradual degradation of a service; disallow new connections
- **integrity services:** protect continued correctness, completeness and 'currentness' of data, applications, etc; detect anomalies, prevent, detect and respond to errors. Examples: full input checking; syntax checking; semantic validation; output validation; virus detection and control
- **confidentiality services:** enforce, protect and support use of confidential information. Examples: enforce classification and labelling and supporting policies
- **cryptographic services:** cryptography to protect confidentiality, validate and demonstrate authenticity and integrity, hide presence of communication

- **hardening services:** monitor and enforce security settings according to policies; detect and report divergence; respond and react to (new) vulnerabilities; patch management.

The security services themselves must be securely managed as well, so the following are needed:
- management and control of security services:
  - monitor correct behavior of security services
  - define points of administration
  - define Change Management with clear acceptance after testing
  - enforce security policy
- ownership and responsibility for managed objects
  - the definition of split or shared responsibilities between service providers and their customers is relevant here. Also, management of trust across a service delivery chain is an issue
- authoritative sources of security information:
  - which are recognized authoritative sources?
  - how are these maintained?
  - example: which model for authorizations is used and enforced?
- detecting and monitoring incidents, events (especially near misses, which provide valuable lessons), vulnerabilities and follow up
  - signalling of intrusions, weaknesses, vulnerabilities and incidents. This may be based on input from trusted internal or external parties, such as a CERT (Computer Emergency Response Team)
- reporting, assurance and compliancy services: evidence of correct behavior as well as evidence that certain levels of performance are or are not met are useful since these reduce the cost to prove compliance. New rules and regulations have put a heavy burden on organizations to not only exceed expectations, but also to provide sufficient assurance that this is indeed the case. The more these processes can be automated, the easier it is. (Note: a simple example of developing maturity is that in the first couple of years, the emphasis will be on demonstrated assurance in the general infrastructure, then on 'proven' assurance provided by applications and finally the emphasis will be on risk management in business-relevant terms.)

These are the common security services; many more exist. For a detailed description see *The Common Criteria for IT Security Evaluation* ISO/IEC 15408.

A service oriented security architecture defines:
- which security services are provided centralized/decentralized
- where services are provided in (which combination of) the supporting architectures:
  - in the data/information architecture
  - in the application architecture
  - in the IT infrastructure architecture
  - in the physical/environmental architecture
- which security mechanisms are mandatory, optional, supported,… and again, the placement of these mechanisms.

For further information about security architectures see the ISO 7498-2 standard.

3 Fundamentals of management of information security

Information Security Management is essentially a series of activities that manages a specified level of security of information and IT. It deals with establishing and maintaining all that is needed to keep the required level of information security. Whether threats from the outside world or changes of business processes, the required level of security has to be maintained to keep business risk at an agreed and acceptable level.

The basis for that required level is the agreed specification of information security. These specifications are laid down in contracts or agreements such as a Service Level Agreement (SLA). ISO/IEC 27002, as a best practice, provides a list of controls to be considered as a starting point, including:

- availability of a corporate information security policy
- description of controls to ensure asset protection
- user and administrator training
- provisions for transfer of personnel
- specifications of the process of change management
- access control policy
- points of contact
- compliance
- details about auditing security
- reporting.

How to reach the required level of information security – that is, how to determine what measures/controls are to be taken – is one part of Information Security Management. It contains subjects such as risk analysis, the definition of appropriate measures, creating a standard minimum level of information security, the implementation of controls and operational monitoring such as intrusion detection.

The other part of Information Security Management deals with maintaining information security at the required level. Subjects include incident registration and handling, trend analysis and reporting, escalation support, maintaining standards, vulnerability management, awareness communication, etc.

When information security is in place, operational and functioning, it is a continuous process. The Information Security Management process coordinates and directs the security activities, using a standard process management cycle.

3.1   Information Security Management – the continuous effort

The management of information security is a continuous effort. This continuous effort concerns the effectiveness of security in everyday operation and comparing that level of effectiveness with the actual control objectives/security requirements. There must be regular evaluation of the goals and targets of information security in order to maintain the required confidence from the business.

But the continuous effort of the management of information security is not only in the operation. It should also be in the transition towards operation, in the design of services and in the strategy for security. A proper feedback loop is needed as well, to enable maintenance or continuous improvement of security.

3.2   Information Security Management as a PDCA cycle

A process approach is adopted to describe the activities that in combination result in Information Security Management. A process is defined as a set of related activities that transforms input to output, uses resources and is managed. This allows use of the well-known PDCA cycle (Plan-Do-Check-Act) to detail functions such as establishing, implementing, operating, monitoring, reviewing and improving of the management of the process. The PDCA cycle is also the basis of ISO/IEC 27001.

3.2.1   Overview
The PDCA cycle, also known as the Deming Cycle [DEM], provides a framework for improvement of a process, although it lacks a controlling function to maintain the momentum. To emphasize the importance of maintaining momentum, a central control function has been added to the model without altering the role and functions of Plan, Do, Check and Act (see figure 3.1).

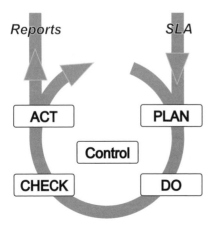

Figure 3.1: The Information Security Management PDCA cycle

The input of Information Security Management consists of the information security requirements stated by all business, partners involved and the service provider itself; the output is the established information security that meets those requirements. Reporting is used to provide evidence of meeting the requirements. The same reporting provides overview information, which is useful in awareness and communication programs for the organization.

Care should be taken when organizations are part of a chain or network. There could be a situation where security in the leading and trailing processes falls outside the scope of this Information Security Management domain; however, consistency over all processes in the chain is necessary to ensure that security is not breached in another part of the chain.

Special consideration is required where multiple SLAs exist. Often the required security levels differ; and different service providers may offer variations in security levels. Information Security Management must be investigated to determine to what extent those variations will create additional security implications. Effective communication on this subject between the parties may well be one of the more challenging activities to organize.

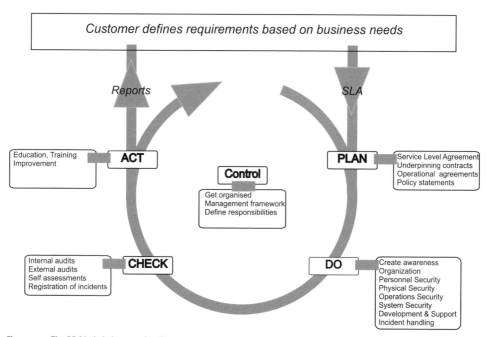

Figure 3.2: The PDCA circle in more detail

3.2.2 CONTROL: Control of Information Security Management
Control of Information Security Management looks like the conundrum 'who manages the manager'. For implementation and functioning of Information Security Management, control is indispensable.

The objective is to organize Information Security Management. It provides the ability to implement and execute Information Security Management in a consistent manner. Without control the results are less predictable and management will not be able to perform as required. Certification of an Information Security Management process will be impossible without control in place.

Summary of activities

The control activity is aligned with the other control processes within IT management. The Information Security Manager (ISM) is the manager of the control activities; this can be a role or a function. The ISM is a peer to his/her fellow process managers.

Control of Information Security Management directs and organizes the Information Security Management process, which includes the organization of the management framework for Information Security Management. Implementation of an Information Security Management process requires planning and procedures. In addition, control enables reporting of status, results and progress.

The control activity defines the (sub)processes, the functions, roles and the responsibilities within those subprocesses. It also identifies the organization and reporting structure.

Management forum

It is important to establish a steering body, providing input from internal and/or external customers. For internal service providers, control of Information Security Management is greatly supported by a management forum for information security. This forum can be composed of the jointly responsible line managers, plus employees with specialist security roles (who can also do the work required to prepare for forum meetings). The forum meets several times a year (for example as part of an extended normal management team meeting) to give direction to information security. The typical tasks of such a forum would be to:
• provide steering
• review the policy, review control objectives
• modify the control framework and security measures
• approve security plans
• maintain responsibilities
• monitor changing threats and incidents.

Input for this forum can come from corporate assurance functions such as a Governance, Risk and Compliance Board or Enterprise Risk Management.
External service providers can also use this approach by organizing customer security interest groups.

Coordination

Another vital part of the control of Information Security Management is the coordination of information security within the organization of the service provider. This refers to:
• implementing plans and measures
• agreements about co-operation and co-ordination between the various roles and responsibilities relating to information security

- agreements about the methods and techniques to be used (for example, the method used for risk analysis and the use of a single classification system throughout the organization)
- setting up organization-wide initiatives (for example a security awareness program).

The coordinating role does not only address operational issues, but also the coordination of other issues including strategy, design, transfer and review.

Security in new IT: testing, acceptance

A major subject of information security is authorization of information processing processes, which includes the authorization process for information services and IT facilities. Before these become operational, they must be tested to ensure that security requirements are met. This requires a process for testing and acceptance. Testing usually implies positive testing (whether a specified input results in a specified output). Security testing also implies negative testing: the absence of unwanted functionality, vulnerability testing, negative impact from/on layered or adjacent infrastructure such as other operating systems or applications, performance under pressure, robustness for input or processing errors and resilience. These aspects should be built into the testing process.

Acceptance of a new service, IT facility or part of the infrastructure is a formal step. It may involve acceptance by the representative of the service user organization.

Specialized advice

Part of Information Security Management is about making decisions in highly technical security matters such as encryption, risks or audits. Specialist advice may be necessary.

Sharing

There is a great deal of co-operation between organizations in the specialist security sector. There are organizations such as the Information Security Forum (ISF – www.securityforum.org), the SANS institute (www.sans.org) or the International Information Integrity Institute (I4 – www.i4online.com) that share experiences and provide best practice information. Not only methods and techniques are discussed; threats, risks and surveys of security controls are also frequently discussed topics.

Independent review

This is another mechanism that supports Information Security Management. It ensures that the implementation of information security is regularly reviewed by an independent party – for example, those of the internal or external IT auditor.

3.2.3 PLAN: Planning within Information Security Management

The starting point of planning is proper organization of information security, which means that responsibilities and authorities are defined and specified at all required levels.

Objective

The objectives of the PLAN sub process are twofold: define/maintain 'to be'-plans and define/maintain the annual cycle for Information Security Management.

Summary of activities

The main activities are defining and maintaining 'to be' plans, together with the annual cycle of information security management activities.

Maintain/define 'to be'-plans

The SLA requirements and control objectives of the customers (as well as those of the service provider) are translated into controls/measures laid down in plans; they are maintained in such a way that the controls/measures remain actual in view of changing risks. These plans typically address the baseline controls and additional controls that reflect the specific risks of an information system; they may also describe typical control activities that are implemented in a process.

Examples are:
- description of risk registers and risk treatment/security improvement plans
- control frameworks or lists of baseline security measures
- templates for reporting
- periodic reviews, assessments, audits and evaluation
- collection of event and incident information, evidence, log files
- description of the crypto key hierarchy and management
- process descriptions for incident, user/authorization and continuity management.

Typical outputs of this sub process are the Information Security Policy and the security baseline. Security service levels can be defined here as well. Customers will be likely to have diverse requirements, but note that a translation of these requirements to the standard baseline or to a small number of security service levels is often possible, which limits the requirement to maintain error-prone specials.

One of the main products of this sub process is the security improvement plan or risk treatment plan in which the improvement activities are laid down and residual risks are accepted.

Annual cycle for Information Security Management

Many Information Security Management activities are planned ahead and executed accordingly. In resource planning, a good practice is to make reservations for ad hoc activities that cannot be planned upfront. Examples of periodic activities are organizing self-assessments, awareness activities, monitoring security in innovation processes, reviews/audits, risk analysis and improvement planning.

3.2.4 DO: Operation of Information Security Management

The operation of Information Security Management means performing the activities required to maintain the level or quality of the organization's information security in the context of the organization's and customers' overall business risks.

Objective

The objective is to executed ad hoc and planned activities in an efficient and effective way that reflects the requirements of the customers as well as the service provider.

Summary of activities

Some activities are continuous processes; some take place several times a year as defined in the annual cycle; and some are projects defined in the Security Improvement Plan that take place as continuous processes.

Examples of continuous processes are:
- security incident handling. Incident handling encompasses a wide range of activities that deal with incidents, from the procedure to report incidents, via registration to coordination of handling the incidents, escalation if required and cooperation with Problem Management and other Support Management
- support of Change Management. Changing requirements or occurrence of security incidents require follow-up by modifying systems, organizations or procedures. For this, the Change Management process is instrumental. Expertise from the information security organization is required to prevent decrease of the security level
- user, identity and authorization management/access management: given the increasing requirements in this area, a common policy and process is needed that guarantees or provides coherence of access rights throughout the organization and for customers
- CERT (computer emergency response team), vulnerability management, patch management
- maintaining awareness. Communication is an activity that does not automatically fit within Information Security Management. However, to maintain momentum, to keep the organization alert as far as information security is concerned, communication is crucial. Only through communication is it possible to prevent the failure of well designed controls because of human failure, neglect or lack of users' willingness to cooperate
- supporting the organization with risk assessments
- supervising reviews and audits. After planning (in the PLAN phase) reviews and audits have to take place. Supervising and supporting the reviews is one of the regular tasks within Information Security Management. Registration of the reviews and filing and reporting on the results are additional tasks.

Implementation of information security controls and the coordination of that implementation can be seen as one of the activities of the operation phase of Information Security Management.

3.2.5 CHECK: Review of Information Security Management

Information security without reviews will not work, because there has to be some means of assessing its effectiveness in operation. There will always be human error or reluctance to follow security procedures. Since security controls and countermeasures require effort or performance, people tend to take the easy way out, forgetting about rules and procedures that are not designed to make work easier.

Different types of reviews can be used. These can range from formal audits, through independent reviews, supervision and self assessments to ' Quick Scans', designed to take a snapshot of the controls in place.

Whether executed by external parties or by the internal auditing department, reviews help to identify if every player is still performing. It is the best instrument to determine where and what to change to maintain the required security level.

Objective: to assess (check) compliance with the information security policy and standards of the service provider and compliance with the agreed objectives, controls and standards of the customers, usually laid down in the SLA. This requires a regular audit of the (technical) security of the information systems. The service provider supplies information for this to an independent auditor or the customer's auditor.

Summary of activities
- undesirable use of information, services or IT facilities: focus on preventing undesirable use or even misuse of the resources placed at the discretion of employees. Only permit use for authorized business objectives, covered by the job description of the employee. The same limitation applies to the use of resources by and of third parties. This includes, for example, not only those activities that may be covered by legislation on computer crime, but also the improper use of IT facilities, such as playing computer games or keeping private accounts. Include in the SLA details of what is expected of the service provider in this area
- compliance with security policy and standards: regularly check compliance with the security policy, the security standards and any other security requirements taking into account the effectiveness and efficiency of the policy and the framework of security measures
- legal compliance, including prevention of illegal copying of software
- security reviews of IT systems: regularly check compliance with the technical security standards for IT facilities
- IT audits: carefully plan and execute the audits in the information processing environment so that the organization and responsibilities are clear; the audit activities are laid down and interference with production is kept to the minimum. The knowledge and level of experience of the IT auditors must be monitored
- audit tools should only be available to authorized employees.

3.2.6 ACT: Maintaining Information Security Management
Security has to be maintained. The reasons to enhance security can come from incidents reports, vulnerability assessments, audits, trends in risks and developments within the market and the customers' business environments.

Risk assessments should be updated as part of risk management on a regular basis. The risks in the outside world as well as within organizations are constantly changing, and controls in place may gradually become obsolete due to developments in IT.

It is advisable to repeat the risk assessments regularly. This is even more important after major changes in infrastructure, in organizational structure, in processes or in operational goals.

Part of the maintenance effort has to be devoted to the descriptions of the 'to be' situation in plans and security handbooks. These descriptions have to be updated.

In this step it is a good practice to register the reasons for maintenance and all actions taken.

Objective

- to improve the 'to be' situation (PLAN). The 'to be' situation includes the agreements on security as specified in SLAs, the internal standards such as the Information Security Policy, the baseline, handbooks and Operational Level Agreements (OLAs), as well as the agreements with the underpinning contracts
- to improve implementation of specified security measures (PLAN, DO)
- to report to the customers on security performance.

Summary of activities

- analysis of the evaluation reports
- providing input for the PLAN sub process, the security plan(s) and the annual improvement activities
- providing input for the SLA maintenance activities (for the Service Level Manager) as well as for the maintenance activities on operational level agreements and underpinning contracts.

Management review as part of Information Security Management

A management review takes place to check the effectiveness and efficiency of the current implementation of controls/measures. The input to the management review should include information on:

- analyses from the collected incidents and vulnerabilities
- feedback from interested parties
- results of independent reviews/audits
- status of preventive and corrective actions
- results of previous management reviews
- process performance and compliance with information security policy
- changes that could affect the organization's approach to managing information security, including changes to the organizational environment, business circumstances, resource availability, contractual, regulatory, and legal conditions, or to the technical environment
- trends related to threats and vulnerabilities
- assessments of third parties/partners/suppliers; information security incidents and status of security
- recommendations provided by relevant authorities.

The output from the management review should include any decisions and actions related to:

- improvement of the organization's approach to managing information security and its processes
- improvement of control objectives and controls
- improvement in the allocation of resources and/or responsibilities.

A record of the management review, clearly stating management involvement and approval, should be maintained.

3.2.7 Reporting

Reporting is an inevitable part of Information Security Management; it is necessary to provide assurance, to give insight on the current status and to account for the current achievements.

Objective

The objective is to provide the customers or the organization with relevant information on information security.

Summary of activities

In general, the Information Security Management process provides reporting data to the Service Level Management process. Service Level Management takes care of the communication with the customer.

Possible regular reports and reportable events are:
- reports on the PLAN sub process:
  - reports on conformance to the SLAs and internal standards including the agreed key performance indicators (KPIs) for security
  - reports on the status of the controls: as long as there is evidence that controls are working, the desired level of security should be met.
  - reports on underpinning contracts and defined non-conformity in their fulfilment
  - reports on OLAs and policy statements
- progress of the security improvement plan and other annual plans
  - regular reports on the DO sub process:
  - status of information security such as implemented measures, education and reviews including self assessments and risk analyses
  - overview of security incidents and the reaction to these incidents, compared to a previous time frame
  - status of awareness programs
  - trends on incidents by system, by process, by department, etc.
- reports on and of the CHECK sub process:
  - results of audits, reviews and internal assessments
  - warnings, vulnerabilities, trends, new threats, et cetera

Specific reportable events:
- for certain security incidents, the Incident Control or Service Desk and the Security Manager should have a direct channel to the customer's representative. This is part of the alerting/escalation procedure, which goes beyond the normal reporting procedures.

4   ITIL version 3 and information security

ITIL version 3 introduction

ITIL's most recent version, version 3, represents an important evolutionary step. The refresh has transformed the guidance from providing a good service to being the most innovative and best in class. At the same time, the interface between old and new approaches is seamless so that users do not have to reinvent anything when adopting it.

Perhaps the strongest single concept in ITIL version 3 is the concept of competition. Every IT service provider faces competition. As many internal service providers have found, they will inevitably be tested against the market. The key for IT service providers is to understand how they provide value and differentiate themselves for their target customers; and for customers it is to understand where they should be best concentrating their efforts, and where shared or external service providers can do things better.

ITIL version 3 allows users to build on the successes of ITIL version 2 but takes IT service management further. In general, ITIL version 3 makes the link between ITIL's best practice and business benefits both clearer and stronger. The main development is that ITIL version 3 takes a lifecycle approach to guidance, whereas ITIL version 2 had a process approach.

The service lifecycle model

In ITIL version 3 it is crucial that service management starts from the lifecycle view of a service: the service lifecycle model. The implementation of a particular process is no longer central (e.g. Incident Management); instead, the main focus is on the continual improvement of the provision of services. Within the service lifecycle model each phase encompasses old (from ITIL version 2) and new processes. The axis or core of the model is Service Strategy, which is the phase of high level goals and objectives. The other phases (Service Design, Service Transition and Service Operation) implement this strategy. However, things do change, which is why the phase of Continual Service Improvement is linked to the other phases. In the service lifecycle model this is shown by placing Continual Service Improvement at the outer edge of the circle. Continual Service Improvement is about improvement programs and projects based on the vision and strategic goals of an organization. Complementary publications and web support services are placed at the rim of the circle.

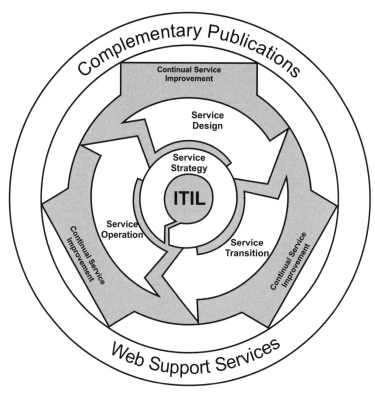

Figure 4.1: The ITIL Service Lifecycle (Crown Copyright)

The ITIL version 3 books

Each ITIL version 3 book deals with a phase of the service lifecycle model:

- Service Strategy
- Service Design
- Service Transition
- Service Operation
- Continual Service Improvement.

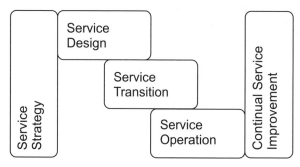

Figure 4.2: The lifecycle phases of ITIL version 3

To show the lifecycle phases in their relationships, figure 4.2 is used. It shows (from left to right) Service Strategy, the overall view of IT from a strategic perspective; Service Design, in which design of the service takes place; Service Transition where the services are transferred to the business environment; Service Operation, which focuses on delivery and control of the services; and finally Continual Service Improvement to maintain and improve the services provided.

Both Service Strategy and Continual Service improvement have relationships with the three phases in the center of figure 4.2.

Service Strategy
This is a view of ITIL that aligns business and IT so that each brings out the best in the other. It ensures that every stage of the service lifecycle stays focused on the business case and relates to all the companion process elements that follow.

In the Service Strategy book the following processes are dealt with:
• Financial Management
• Service Portfolio Management
• Demand Management.

Service Design
In order to meet the current and future business requirements, Service Design provides guidance on the production and maintenance of IT policies, architectures, and the design of appropriate and innovative IT services solutions and processes.

In the Service Design book the following processes are dealt with:
• Service Level Management (also dealt with in Continual Service Improvement)
• Service Catalog Management
• Supplier Management
• Capacity Management
• Availability Management
• IT Service Continuity Management
• Information Security Management.

Service Transition
Service Transition focuses on the broader, long-term change management role and release practices, so that risks, benefits, delivery mechanism and the ease of ongoing operations of service are considered. This publication provides guidance and process activities for the transition of services into the business environment.

In this book the following processes are dealt with:
• Service Transition Planning and Support
• Change Management
• Service Asset and Configuration Management
• Release and Deployment Management
• Service Validation and Testing
• Evaluation
• Knowledge Management.

Service Operation

By focusing on delivery and control process activities, a steady state of managing services can be achieved on a day-to-day basis. To ensure it is integrated with the rest of the ITIL series, guidance is based on a selection of familiar service support and service delivery control points.

In this book the following processes are dealt with:
• Event Management
• Request Fulfilment
• Incident Management
• Problem Management
• Access Management.

Continual Service Improvement (CSI)

Alongside the delivery of consistent, repeatable process activities as part of service quality, ITIL has always emphasized the importance of continual improvements. Focusing on the process elements involved in identifying and introducing service management improvements, this publication also deals with issues surrounding service decommissioning.

In this book the following processes are dealt with:
• the seven steps model
• Service Reporting
• Service Measurement.

Overview of ITIL version 3

The content of ITIL version 3 is much more complex than ITIL version 2: it now consists of 25 processes and four functions compared to eleven processes and one function in ITIL version 2. The four functions are:
• the Service Desk
• Monitor and Control
• IT Operations (in the book Service Operation)
• Capacity Management (Service Design).

Figure 4.3 gives an overview of all the processes in ITIL version 3; the new processes are in bold type.

Information Security Management and ITIL

Information Security Management is primarily discussed in the Service Design and Service Operation volumes. That is not the complete coverage of the topic: Information Security Management relies on the results of processes outside those two lifecycle phases as well.

Information Security Management does not manage operational processes, so it can be considered as operating on a tactical level. Security of information and information processing is not treated as a tangible product. Information security is embedded, integrated or intrinsically present in the majority of the processes described in ITIL, and this is ensured by the Information Security Management process.

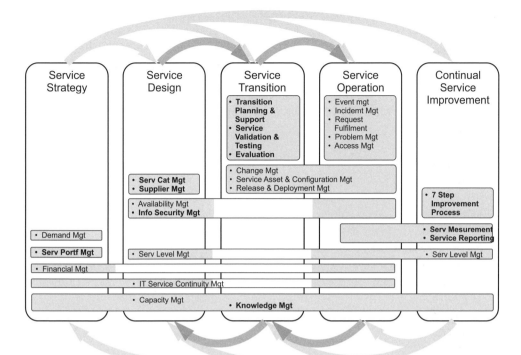

Figure 4.3: ITIL processes as described in ITIL documents

The lifecycle phases are discussed in the following paragraphs. For each phase, the processes are given and the relationship with Information Security Management is explained.

4.1 Service Strategy

Over time, many methods and techniques for organizational control have emerged, also as a result of national and international rules and regulations. Customers are no longer satisfied with a service provider that (only) meets their expectations, but also require their service providers to provide proof that the agreed control objectives and controls are effective and operational.

The relationship between customers and service providers has evolved considerably. In the past, the customer simply had to trust its service providers. Nowadays, customers demand more assurance.

For service providers, being in a competitive market, all the activities they perform should add value in some way to their business. So, resources allocated to security contribute either to the service provider's own security and/or are assigned in such a way that cost reduction is achieved, or contribute to the customer's requirements. The latter is the focus of ITIL Information Security Management.

The business's information risk and security management can benefit from and build upon ITIL's Service Strategy in many ways. Service Strategy is about looking ahead, and indeed looks further than the day-to-day operational issues. The focus is more on partnerships, building mutually beneficial relationships, and the definition of new or renewed services, also to support security.

Without trying to be exhaustive, the most important possible contributions of Service Strategy to Information Security Management and their placement within the recognized processes within Service Strategy are:
- Service Strategy:
  - security strategy
  - maturity level for security
  - assurance issues – risk, auditing and compliance
  - demand-supply relationship in Risk Management
  - principles for security service design and security architectures
- Service Portfolio Management
  - security service portfolio
- Demand Management:
  - security baseline
  - security service proposition
- Financial Management/service economics:
  - Return On Security Investments (ROSI)

These topics are explored further in the following subsections.

4.1.1   Service Strategy Management

Service Strategy Management addresses fundamental questions about the current and future markets, customers and services, such as: why does our business exist today and tomorrow?

Service Strategy support for Information Security Management

Service Strategy can contribute to Information Security Management and Information Risk Management in several ways. Topics addressed in this section are:
- security strategy
- maturity level for security
- risk management and alignment with business risks
- principles for security architectures.

Security strategy

Customers' requirements for Information Security Management are varied. Service providers who tend to accept all or widespread variations in customer requirements have a major task to implement and demonstrate that the requirements are effective. Another option for service providers is to state upfront (taking the current and desired customers' general requirements into account) that compliance to a defined set of standards is aimed for, and that assurance is provided in a defined way. Looking more closely at some of the more common standards in Information Security Management, it is clear that the differences between these standards are not significant, and seldom fundamental. Service providers will benefit if a clear strategy is chosen to adopt one or just a few of the commonly used standards for security and risk management. When clearly communicated to their customers and specific market segments, this approach will circumvent many questions, help to standardize the service offering, reduce cost and probably achieve a better overall result than trying to comply with many (perhaps even customer specific) standards.

The strategic perspective on Information Security Management begins with understanding the value of information risk and security management for the current and future customers and markets. How does Information Security Management provide value, how can this be captured, and how does this quality act as a differentiator to the market and customers? Information Security Management can be a strategic asset. For example, when it is a core competence in a specific market, it provides distinctive performance and advantage, and helps in the development of business opportunities for customers as well as for the service provider itself.

In developing the security strategy, questions to be answered are:
- what security should we offer and to whom?
  - what are the customer and market requirements?
  - what is the potential value to the stakeholders?
  - what should the business case look like?
- how is security a differentiator from competing alternatives?
- how does security create value for our customers? Can we capture this value and turn it into added value both for the customer and for ourselves?
- can we develop a business case to justify strategic investments in security?
- can financial management provide visibility and control over value creation of investments in security and/or security services?
- how should we define the service quality of security? How much transparency in the service offering is required and what quality assurance is suitable?
- how do we choose between different paths for further improving the security of our services?
- how should the baseline for security be defined and managed, as well as the portfolio of security services?

Key elements in the strategy development are:
- the risks that need to be taken into account
- the control objectives that are relevant
- which security standards (control frameworks such as the Code of Practice for Information Security Management, COBIT, PCI) should be adhered to
- what assurance is to be given.

These elements have to be assessed from the customer perspective, taking into account the service provider's ambitions for its customers and markets.

Having answered these questions, additional questions follow naturally:
- which organizational structure (as well as roles and responsibilities) is required to deploy the strategy? Is a security office needed and/or a dedicated Corporate or Chief Information Security Officer (CISO)?
- what is the high level layout of the Information Security Management process?

Maturity level for security

Service providers may choose to be in the market for services ranging from 'standard services with large volumes' to 'customer-tailored services with limited volumes' and anything in between. The positioning of the services may also imply a specific maturity level. In this section, one of the earliest maturity models [NOL] is used freely to sketch this approach (figure 4.4). It is easy to understand and all other models, all having their specific benefits, can be mapped to this simple model.

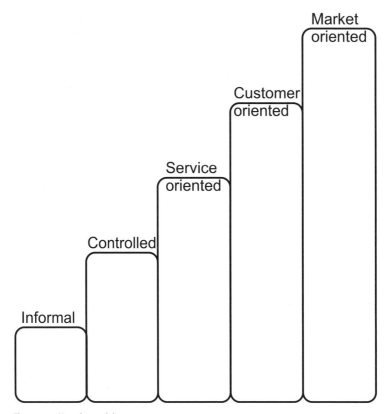

Figure 4.4: Maturity model

Table 4.1 summarizes the maturity levels and their interpretation for Information Security Managemeny.

Maturity level	Importance of IT and information	Typical for security	Type of companies
Informal/ad hoc (techno-logy driven)	IT and use of information sources is of limited importance	Backup and Incident Management	Small and medium enter-prises; not depending on IT; small shops.
Controlled	Highly standard IT use and services	Baseline set of controls or control objectives. Ad-here to external/industry standards	Service providers with standardized services for a wide range of organiza-tions or consumers. E.g. housing of hosting. Organizations with standard use of IT and no high security demands for information.
Service oriented	Reliability of specific services, e.g. email or In-ternet, is a discriminator.	Service-specific risk analyses. Provider focused information risk management. KPIs focus on service-security and SLAs.	Service providers with common services for wide and common use. E.g. email, internet use, payroll provision, HR management. Clients of these standardized services, often seen as supporting facilities.
Customer oriented	Crucial and specific for each customer	Information Risk Management takes the customer's risks into ac-count. Common risk and security processes bet-ween the service provider and the customer.	Service providers for a specific type of customers, e.g. banks or government. Internal service providers.
Market oriented	Information and IT risks are of vital impact for the core business	Information Risk Ma-nagement is focused on the market and/or customer groups in the market. The aim is to offer confidence in the market. Compliance is based on external rules and regulations. Over-sight is organized in the market.	Organizations of syste-matic importance for the market – for example dominant players in the IT-provision or individual banks whose trustworthy-ness affects the whole financial market.

Table 4.1: Maturity levels and their interpretation for information security management

Assurance issues – risk, auditing and compliance

Assurance that a certain level of security is reached comes from a small group of activities. The main activities are risk management, auditing and compliance:

- **risk management** is the process of assessment of the 'likelihood and impact of unwanted events' (risk assessment), risk treatment (elimination, mitigation, acceptance, transfer) and any associated management
- **auditing** is the independent verification of whether defined internal policies or common external standards are met

- **compliance** is conformance with defined standards. Compliance is often used in the context of meeting the requirements from external rules and regulations and management confirmation that these requirements have been met.

The type of assurance management that fits the information service provider best depends on the maturity level of the service provider.

- In the **ad hoc/informal** phase, risk management does not exist. The organization simply reacts to incidents.
- In the **controlled** phase, risk management is merely a matter of checking whether the baseline is properly implemented. A checklist, e.g. the appendix to ISO/IEC 27001, is one of the major instruments in the Information Security Manager's toolkit. Not meeting certain controls of the baseline is seen as a risk So, risk management in this phase does not address business risks or service risks. Auditing is about checking whether the baseline is properly documented and implemented. Compliance reports on conformance with the baseline. The standards that can be used as a baseline are comparable. The Code of Practice for Information Security Management (ISO/IEC 27002) is a good example, with supporting standards, such as ISO/IEC 27004 for metrics and ISO/IEC 27005 to describe the process for risk management.
- In the **service oriented** phase, risk management concentrates on the services offered and their associated risks. These are either risks that are inherent to the service (e.g. viruses and email) or risks for the service provider itself. Auditing may focus on risk management as the auditable object; compliance reports on the risk management process.
- In the **customer oriented** phase, a risk management process between the service provider and customer exists. The service provider is aware of the risks, has formulated control objectives and, based on audits, provides customer-specific compliance reports/evidence about the security performance for this customer.
- Finally in the **market oriented** phase, risk management takes the interests of a sector as the starting point. For example, trust in individual banks is needed for the whole banking sector. The objectives of risk management are often dictated by an oversight organization. Auditing is done against their external and sector specific standards and compliance reporting serves the interest of the overseeing authorities and may serve other external stakeholders as well.

Examples of generally accepted practices that may be used as a foundation are: COBIT and Code of Practice for Information Security Management. Supporting standards are CMM, ISO/IEC 20000 and PRINCE2.

Examples of generally accepted risk management standards are: Management of Risk (M_o_R), AS/NZS 4360 Risk Management and ISO/IEC 27005. Examples of methods for risk assessment are Preservation Risk Management (PRISM), ISF's Information Risk Analysis Methodology (IRAM) and CCTA Risk Analysis and Management Method (CRAMM). Many of these methods are supported with tools. Tools may be useful and help to maintain a reference level throughout the organization; but a tool should never become a goal in itself. A recommended approach is to first perform risk assessments without the assistance of any tools and decide on tooling later.

In the communication between customers and service providers, a good starting point is to communicate which standards are used in each organization.

Demand-supply relationship in risk management

Figure 4.5 shows how alignment of risk management between the customer and service provider can be achieved.

Figure 4.5: Service Management as risk filter

Figure 4.6 shows that risks flow two ways: demand side risks come from the business requirements, supply side risks come from the service provider. Service Management provides the channel to communicate about risks between the service provider and the business.

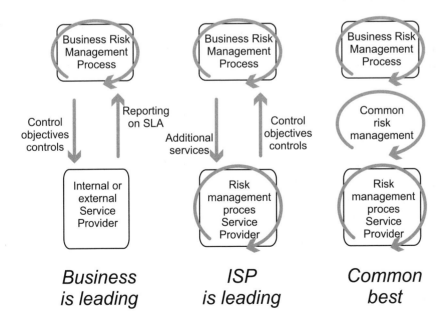

Figure 4.6: Towards a demand/supply relationship in Risk Management

In figure 4.6, the left side of the model sketches the situation where the customer ('business') is leading. As a result of the business's risk management process, control objectives and possibly even controls are dictated to the service provider. The service provider in turn reports on compliance, which should be agreed in the SLA. Since the service provider has no knowledge of the risks of the business, compliance reporting is cumbersome: the service provider reports without knowing the effects of non-compliance. In practice, once the service provider has accepted the business's demands, full compliance is the target. The business can dictate its requirements to all service providers in the same way. The service providers have to tailor the way of working for each individual customer. This is typical for a relationship where the 'business' is a major international company, being served by many service providers, where information and IT are important for the business.

In the middle section of the model, the service provider communicates compliance with its baseline, control objectives and possibly controls to all customers. The service provider has made this selection based on its ambition for its markets and its customers. The business takes this as input for its own risk management process, and may ask for additional services or adapt its internal way of working. The service provider can standardize its way of working. This is typical for a situation where the service provider offers common services that benefit from standardization. This situation is easy for the service provider, but the business has to accept and absorb the resulting risks.

On the right-hand side of the model, a common risk management process is established. Where the above two models, in practice, result in static objectives that slowly evolve over time, the right-hand model provides opportunities to react to risks. Both partners agree on one or a limited set of common standards. Risk reporting goes both ways. Accompanying control objectives are defined by the 'risk receiving party', and on effectiveness of controls communication takes place.

Note that shared processes between service provider and customer are common. Other examples are incident and escalation management, continuity management and authorization management.

Principles for security service design and security architectures

A security architecture defines which security services are offered in the infrastructure and where they occur.

In 'Service Design' the subject of security architectures is elaborated upon. Guiding principles for designing secure environments [SAL] are:
- isolation
- safe defaults
- complete mediation
- open design
- separation of duties
- limited functionality
- compartments
- ergonomics
- redundancy
- diversity.

Note that ITIL version 3 complementary guidance on IT architectures is to be published.

4.1.2 Service portfolio management

The service portfolio describes a provider's services in terms of business value. It articulates business needs and the provider's response to those needs. The business value terms correspond to marketing terms, providing a means for comparing service competitiveness across alternative providers.

Service portfolio management support for Information Security Management: the security service portfolio

An important element in the strategy is the process for maintaining the service portfolio for security.

Key questions are:
- what are the security demands of our current or targeted customers/markets?
- what should we offer as a minimum (without this minimum, customers will go elsewhere and prospects will be lost)?
- what can we offer in addition?
- why should customers buy services with integrated security or specific security services from us?

In general, the portfolio exists in two parts:
- baseline security services: these are the services that are offered as part of the standard service provision. No additional fees apply. Depending on the targeted/current customer base, this baseline could exist as:
  - the Code of Practice for Information Security Management (ISO/IEC 27002)
  - Control Objectives for IT (COBIT)
  - market specific baselines, e.g. Payment Card Industry standards, data protection standards, standards from oversight bodies, etc.
- specific security services: these are the services that a customer can ask for in addition to the standard services, against an additional fee. Examples are:
  - managed security services
  - identity and access management
  - intrusion detection and prevention
  - security incident and event monitoring
  - security operating centers
  - Computer Emergency Response Teams (CERT)
  - business continuity services
  - hardening, penetration testing, etc.

Note that proactive communication about the security offered can be an important selling point. This can be strengthened by also defining the way in which assurance is given. Examples are:
- quarterly reports on incidents
- management confirmation: a statement by the service provider's management about compliance with a certain standard now and in the future
- internal audit reports: assurance given by the service provider's own internal auditors

- certification: certification of security based on commonly accepted standards is possible, for example based on the Code of Practice for Information Security Management
- third party confirmation/external audit reports: a statement by an independent auditor about compliance with an agreed standard. SAS-70 or ISAE 3402 are examples of standards for third party confirmation.

A service provider may choose to include a certain assurance level in its baseline, and add the possibility for additional assurance to the portfolio. For example, certification is part of the baseline since it serves all the customers, but a customer-specific third party assessment is an additional service.

4.1.3 Demand Management

Demand Management is the process of proactive analysis of the customer's requirements for services and resources and planning ahead to either be prepared for these requirements or to influence the customer's demand through financial or other incentives. Demand Management helps to optimize the effective use of resources (Capacity Management), optimize the profits (Cost Management) and steer demands based on financial or other incentives.

Demand Management support for Information Security Management

Demand Management clearly supports availability and continuity. It can also contribute to Information Security Management by clearly communicating with the customers what the service provider supplies. Risks, control objectives and controls can thus be seen from a demand/supply perspective. When the service provider clearly states the supply options, the demand side (the customer organization) will be channelled towards the same path.

Security baseline

Demand Management for Information Security Management includes clearly communicating which standards serve as a reference. Examples of accepted standards include the Code of Practice for Information Security Management (ISO/IEC 27002) and COBIT. The standard for risk management can also be used for reference.

A security baseline is a very useful approach for identifying appropriate security control objectives and designing security controls to meet those objectives. In summary, the baseline concept is as follows:

- the organization looks broadly at its information security risks and identifies a suite of common security controls that are most likely required as a minimum set protecting essentially all information assets (e.g. selecting baseline controls from those identified in ISO/IEC 27002 and/or other generally accepted good security practices)
- those minimal controls are formally described and mandated by management through policies, standards, procedures and guidelines
- the controls are implemented across-the-board, and suitable compliance activities are implemented to ensure this is done properly and comprehensively
- any exceptions to the mandatory baseline controls (e.g. technical constraints on a certain platform or application system) must be handled formally, ideally by an independent risk-based review followed by an informed management decision on whether to accept the exception for a limited time (in which case the relevant information asset owner is held

explicitly accountable for the increased residual risks arising, and a process is implemented to review the risk at some defined future point) or to refuse the exception (and typically invest in improved security)
- additional security controls are added to, or rather build upon, the baseline where justified by the risks affecting particular information assets, whether using classification as a mechanism to link standard sets of controls or by bespoke security design.

Security service proposition
The key consideration in Demand Management for Information Security Management is to differentiate between the standard security that is provided in the security baseline and additional security-related services for which there is an additional charge. The baseline should be chosen to reflect the service provider's strategic objectives and tailored to the current or targeted customers/ markets. In the security service proposition the additional security services should also be present.

4.1.4 Financial management/service economics
Financial Management provides the business and IT with quantification, in financial terms, of the value of IT services, the assets underlying the provision of those services, and the qualification of operational forecasting.

Financial management/service economics support for Information Security Management
Information Security is to be regarded in terms of value for the business and value as part of a service.

Financial management is an increasingly important factor in decision-making about where and which investments are made. Security should be an indivisible quality in each proposal for investments; at the same time, there are investments specific for security. The latter will follow the same route as other investment proposals, and require the same justification. Security professionals will have to become accustomed to the financial negotiation that nowadays is a part of decision making. Information security is added value for the business and this should be justified in financial terms as well. Of course, financial validation for security has inherent limitations; the crux is that these limitations should be made clear.
Note that security services might also have a commercial value in their own right (e.g. spam, malware and content filtering as optional extras on email services).

The pricing of security is the cost-to-value translation necessary to achieve clarity and influence the demand and consumption of services. The security baseline is **not** part of this exercise. The baseline is considered as the level of security that is a 'must have'. This 'must have'-level depends on the current and targeted customers. Cost recovery is done by a 'percentage' on all the services. For security propositions above the baseline, normal commercial validation applies.

Example: The baseline for performing backups is once a week. This baseline is set based on an analysis of the requirements of new customers. This is seen as a 'enabler' for new prospects. The value for the customers of performing a backup every day is roughly the difference between 'at most one week's work is lost' and 'at most one day's work is lost'. This represents a financial benefit. The service provider calculates its additional internal costs for performing extra backups and the margins for a profitable add-on service emerge. The chance that this backup facility is needed by the customer can be added to the cost model, but in reality the customer will act on its perception of whether this is a fair price for this service.

In the 'Service Strategy' book, the use of the Business Impact Assessment is explained, as well as the different cost factors.

Return on Security Investment (ROSI)

There are many methods for making decisions on investments; Total Cost of Ownership (TCO) and Return on Investment (ROI) are widely used. Here ROSI, for Return on Security Investments, is used. ROI is defined as the net profit of an investment divided by the net worth of the assets invested. 'Profit' is either 'additional revenues' or 'less costs'. The resulting percentage is applied to either additional top-line revenue or the elimination of bottom-line cost. Security professionals are used to justifying the investments in security to reduce the risks (likelihood multiplied by impact), thus 'less costs'. For many security professionals the concept of 'create additional revenues' is a new dimension in their thinking.

Organizations investing in IT realize that accompanying investments in governance, risk management and information security are needed. The risk assessment is the key to the definition of control objectives and selection of controls (security measures and activities). However, are the controls effective, and deliver investments (costs) sufficient revenues (benefits) for the organization, compared to 'doing nothing'? And how should the set of controls be balanced? Should a preventive set of controls be sought, or is a set of controls aiming at detection and correction the better choice?

Central questions are:
- what is the value of information?
- what value is lost due to (the impact of) an incident?
- what is the likelihood of the incident occurring?
- what is the repair cost?
- what is the cost of implementing controls?
- what is the cost of maintaining controls?

ROSI can be used for investments that are not 'must haves' but 'additional value'. It makes proposals comparable, with a comparable margin of error.

A well known cost model is the Annual Loss Expectancy:

R = L * I
      Risk = Likelihood * Impact

Or

ALE = $\sum$ (ARO * SLE) = SUM (ARO * SLE)
      ALE: Annual Loss Exposure/expectancy
      ARO: Expected Annual Rate of Occurrence

SLE: Single Loss Exposure, the Financial impact
ALE = Sum of all incidents of (Annual Rate of Occurrence * Single Loss Exposure)

Informally:

ALE = SUM (likelihood of the incident * impact of the incident)

This sum (SUM) considers all anticipated incidents per year. Impact is expressed as direct costs plus repair costs for repair.

Note that the ALE should be calculated over the value chain; for example: infrastructure provider + housing provider + hosting provider + application service provider + customer + customers of the customer. A security incident at one point in the chain causes disruptions across all of the chain.

Do controls provide sufficient benefits? That depends on the reduction of the ALE, expressed as $ALE_{old} - ALE_{new}$. Investments (C) are split into single investments (C_{inv}), and yearly operational costs, C_{year}, (management, licenses, lifecycle updates). In this example we assume that the investments will be effective for three years.

The formula is as follows:

$$C_{inv}/3 + C_{year} < ALE_{old} - ALE_{new}$$

In formulating business cases, the question is: which are the options or alternatives? Do other possibilities exist to achieve the same risk reduction? What benefits are achievable when the investments are allocated differently? What is the ROI on an investment in, say, an awareness program compared to the same investment in, e.g. disaster recovery?

What makes ROSI different from ROI is that the return can be either increased revenues or cost reduction. In the assessment subjective factors, such as awareness and likelihood of incidents are also of importance.

In Financial Management ROI represents the calculated profit as a percentage of invested capital.

The definition of ROI and ROSI is:

ROSI = (Benefits – Costs)/Costs

Or

ROSI = [(RiskExposure * %RiskMitigation) – C]/ C

And, adding the ALE:

ROSI = [(ALE$_{old}$ – ALE$_{new}$) – C)]/ C

In the formula, the time factor is absent. In calculating the ROI, the period over which the benefits and the costs are taken should be the same.

In the business case, the costs and the benefits are specified. Costs include direct and yearly costs for operation, management and maintenance (lifecycle updates). Benefits include objective profits (more sales, less incidents, higher availability, less claims, less wasted hours, reduced full-time equivalent (FTE) count) and subjective benefits (image, 'trust' of society, political impact, improved security culture).

> Security professionals must span the boundary between IT and the business. Incidents may appear in the IT arena, but their impact is on the customer's business. The issue is not about technical failure, but about loss of the customer's production or data. To define security impact in business terms, define the KPIs for the business of the customers and assess the impact of the investments in security for these KPIs.

Decisions about investment proposals will only partly be based on ROSI. Other factors that are often seen include:
• compliance with industry standards by benchmarking
• investments needed to maintain the baseline level of security
• based on the best ROI
• fits the policy of the organization.

ROI does not stand alone, but is part of the innovation process in which investment proposals are accepted or rejected. A PRINCE2 business case model, part of the Project Initiation Documentation, is often used.

4.2   Service Design

If services or processes are not designed they will evolve organically. If they evolve without proper controls, the tendency is to simply react ad hoc to incidents with patchwork where a proper design would be beneficial based on a clear understanding of the overall vision and overall needs of the business. It is unlikely that any improvement program will ever be able to achieve the same results as proper design would achieve in the first place.

The main aim of Service Design is to design IT services, together with the governing IT practices, processes and policies to realize the strategy and to facilitate the introduction of these services into the live environment, ensuring quality service delivery, customer satisfaction and cost effective service provision. In relation to Information Security Management one of the goals is to design secure and resilient IT services, IT infrastructures, environments, applications and data information resources as well as the processes for their secure management and capability that meet the current and future needs of the business and customers. To emphasize the role of security, the Information Security Management process is described within this ITIL volume of Service Design.

The scope of Service Design is not limited to new services. It includes the changes and improvements necessary to increase or maintain value to customers over the lifecycle of services, the continuity of services, achievement of service levels, and conformance to standards and regulations.

Service Design should fit into the framework set out by Service Strategy. This part of the service lifecycle designs the Information Security Management services, aligned with the business objectives and other goals of Service Strategy. One of the main points is that Service Design should address the risks already identified, eliminate or mitigate them or at least make them explicit. Security requirements from legislation and compliance should also be taken into account into the design of the services.

The concept of service lifecycle management is an architectural principle. The design of a service is not a one-time phase. Continual improvement should be embedded in all Service Design activities to ensure that the solutions and designs become more effective over time and to identify changing trends in the business that may offer opportunities for improvement. Designing to match an anticipated environment can be more effective and efficient, but is often impossible when the future is hard to predict; hence the need to consider flexible, iterative and incremental approaches, also referred to as evolutionary design principles, to Service Design.

It is important that a holistic approach to all aspects of design is adopted and that all other aspects are considered when changing or amending any of the individual elements of design. Thus when designing and developing a new application, it should not be done in isolation, but should also consider the impact on the overall service, the Service Portfolio and Service Catalog, the technology, the Service Management processes and the necessary measurements and metrics. In the design phase a service could first be launched at a simple level and in future releases evolve into a more sophisticated service. For example, a service could start with just password security; later on the service could be combined with a smartcard with biometrics as an option. Which service has to be developed under rigorous security requirements and which services do not need such protection depends on the guidelines and outcomes of Service Strategy and, in particular, Service Portfolio Management.

In the Service Design book the following processes are dealt with:
- Service Level Management
- Service Catalog Management
- Supplier Management
- Capacity Management
- Availability Management
- IT Service Continuity Management
- Information Security Management.

These processes and their relationship with security are described in the following paragraphs.

4.2.1 Service Level Management
Service Level Management ensures that agreements about the services supplied to customers are specified and fulfilled. The goal is to create an IT service of the optimum level: that is, the wishes and requirements of the customers of the IT services are fulfilled and the associated costs can be justified for both the IT service provider and the customer.

The SLAs must also include agreements about the control objectives to be met and, possibly, controls/security measures to be taken.

Service Level Management makes a distinction between a number of connected activities that have to be examined from the security point of view:
- identification of the security requirements and wishes of the customer
- verification of the feasibility of these security requirements and the wishes of the customer
- negotiation of proposals and recording of the required level of security of the IT services
- determining, drawing up and establishing security standards for the IT service
- monitoring these security standards
- monitoring the security aspects within the underpinning contracts (together with Supplier Management)
- reporting on the effectiveness and status of security of IT services provided.

The starting point when establishing the SLA is often that a general level of security exists (the basic level of security, or baseline). It must be explicitly laid down in the SLA if a customer wants a higher level of security.

Security is one of the elements of fitness for use or warranty of every service. Security, with its aspects of confidentiality, availability and integrity, is an implicit psychological component of every service delivered. In most cultures, the service provider must at least offer a level of security based on normal practices and 'housekeeping'. To avoid the impact of cultural differences, it is of the utmost importance that a SLA makes explicit the implicit security needs of the business as far as possible.

4.2.2 Service Catalog Management
In classic ITIL this process and its activities were part of Service Level Management. The goal of the Service Catalog Management (SCM) process is to ensure that a Service Catalog is produced and maintained, containing accurate information on all operational services as well as those being developed for operational use. A Service Catalog may exist in two forms:

- **Business Service Catalog**: all IT services delivered to the customers, the relationships with the business units and the business processes that are dependent on the IT service. This is the customer perspective
- **Technical Service Catalog:** all IT services delivered to the customers, the relationships with the supporting services, other Configuration Items (CIs) needed to support the service. This is the technical perspective

In both forms, the security aspects should be part of the description of the service from a functional and respectively technical point of view. Both depend on a Business Impact Analysis, which should provide information on the impact, priority and risk associated with each service as well as changes to service requirements.

4.2.3 Supplier Management
This process is new in ITIL version 3. The goal of the Supplier Management process is to manage suppliers and the services they supply, to provide seamless quality of IT service to the business, ensuring value for money is obtained. It is essential that supplier management processes and planning are involved in all stages of the service lifecycle from strategy and design through transition and operation to improvement. Complex business demands require the complete

scope of capabilities and resources to support provision of a comprehensive set of IT services, so the use of suppliers and the services they provide are an integral part of any end-to-end solution. Suppliers and the management of suppliers and partners are essential to the provision of quality IT services.

Supplier Management makes a distinction between a number of connected activities that have to be examined from the security point of view:
- ensure that underpinning contracts and agreements with suppliers are aligned to business security needs and support and align with agreed targets in Service Level Requirements (SLRs) and SLAs, in conjunction with Service Level Management
- manage the relationships with suppliers that provide security services
- manage supplier security performance
- manage the security aspects with the Supplier and Contract Database
- negotiate and agree the security elements of the contracts with suppliers and manage this through their lifecycle
- audit.

The security policy of a supplier is one of the most neglected parts of IT service provision. It should be aligned with the security policy of the IT service provider. In practice, security policies may differ in scope, severe and detail. It should be made clear upfront which security service is provided and what 'guarantee' (assurance) the supplier can offer that their services are secure. One of the selection criteria for an external supplier could be whether they are ISO/IEC 27001 certified.

4.2.4 Capacity Management

Capacity Management is responsible for the optimum deployment of IT resources, as agreed with the customer. The performance requirements are derived from the qualitative and quantitative standards that are drawn up in the Service Level Management process.

Most of the activities in the Capacity Management process are related to Information Security Management:
- **Business Capacity Management:** this activity translates the security requirements of the business into security requirements for the services and the IT infrastructure
- **Service Capacity Management:** this activity manages and predicts the end-to-end performance of the services. It monitors and improves performance in terms of throughput capacity and response times. This activity can provide a great deal of information, which, when analyzed, may reveal security incidents
- **Component Capacity Management:** this activity provides an insight into the IT infrastructure and its use. Monitoring data storage space may, for example, provide information about the storage of undesirable data. Assessing new technologies from the point of view of security may reveal some useful information. In practice, one determines and monitors what a system processes as a result of the processing of applications. Significant departures from the normal daily workload may indicate security incidents, although not necessarily
- **Demand Management:** if the demand for capacity is spread out, a decision may be taken to establish certain extra security requirements, or alternatively to reduce them to a baseline level. Business demands should be viewed from a short term and long term perspective

- **application sizing:** estimates the resources required for an application. If these specifications are not available, it will sometimes be necessary to turn to suppliers. The specifications they provide should always be checked for accuracy and the security risks involved
- **modeling and trend information:** models make it possible to set up a number of security scenarios and to make various 'what if' analyses.
- **threshold management:** to implement and manage certain security thresholds can help in determining possible bottlenecks and issues. Thresholds may trigger an alarm, which should be dealt with by Incident and Event Management
- **new technology:** security aspects should be part of the selection criteria for new technology. Care should also be taken when deploying new technology (e.g. new type of servers) to determine to what extent security functionality is built in as a default.

4.2.5 Availability Management

Availability Management is concerned with the technical availability of IT components. It manages the information security in terms of the availability criterion. The quality aspect of availability is guaranteed by other quality aspects: reliability, maintainability, serviceability and resilience. The reliability of an IT service indicates the degree to which the service offers the agreed functionality during an indicated period. Maintainability is an indication of the ease with which maintenance can be carried out on a service, on the basis of prescribed methods and techniques. Serviceability of an IT service means the way in which contracts with third parties about the availability of their IT components are dealt with. Resilience is the ability of an IT service to continue to operate properly, in spite of the malfunctioning of one or more subsystems.

Clearly, Availability Management is closely connected with Information Security Management: breach of an agreed IT service level, for example when an IT service is not available, may be caused by a security incident. The vital business functions should highlight the business critical parts of a business process that are supported by a service. Some IT components may have a classification of 'zero fault tolerance' which means that the availability should be as high as possible and that no other IT component can replace it. The security of such a component should be carefully investigated. Analysis of single-points-of-failure (SPOF) also reveals critical components.

4.2.6 IT Service Continuity Management

This process ensures that, whatever incident or disaster occurs, its consequences for IT services are limited to a level agreed with the customer. With the ever-increasing dependency on IT, it is important that IT services are consistently delivered to an agreed level of quality. Every time a service is degraded or unavailable, customers are unable to continue with their normal business, so it is important that the effects of losing the use of IT systems is assessed.

This is why it is imperative that contingency plans are made in order to ensure the continued operation of the business and also to provide the ability to successfully recover IT services in the event of a disaster or if a major vulnerability is identified. The contingency plan also gives clear guidance on how and when this plan should be invoked.

4.3   Service Transition

Service Transition is at the center of the ITIL lifecycle structure. It may not be readily apparent that successfully moving from the concept of 'how' (developed by design) into 'what' (as supported by operations) is going to be the key element of delivering the required business support. Service Transition concentrates on delivering the service vision in a relevant and cost-effective way; it is defined by the service design concepts that supply its inputs and the Service Operations expectations that serve as its outputs – which are the usable services. The best way of achieving Service Transition will vary between organizations and has to reflect the risks, resources and other parameters relating to that organization in general and the service in transition in particular. Service Transition is needed because business environments are in a constant state of transition. The quest for competitive advantage, best-of-breed innovation and self-preservation are never-ending catalysts for change.

The main purpose of Service Transition is to plan and manage the capabilities and resources required to package, build, test and deploy a release into production and to establish the service specified in the customer and stakeholder requirements. Service Transition is supported by underlying principles that evolve from Service Strategy considerations and underpin the Service Transition practices and approach.

All services should be considered for their potential impact on relevant security concerns, and subsequently tested for their actual likely impact on security. Any service that has an anticipated security impact or exposes an anticipated security risk will have been assessed at the design stage, and the requirement for security management involvement built into the service package.

In the Service Transition book the following processes are dealt with:
• Change Management
• Service Asset and Configuration Management
• Release and Deployment Management
• Service Transition Planning and Support
• Service Validation and Testing
• Evaluation
• Knowledge Management.

4.3.1   Change Management

From the security point of view, the Change Management process is one of the most important processes. This is where new security measures are introduced into the IT infrastructure and existing measures are refined, along with the changes to the IT infrastructure. It is also where checks are made that other changes to systems are implemented without compromising the existing security environment.

Change Management is a key process in Service Transition and serves the whole service lifecycle. The goal of the Change Management process is to react to the ever-changing business of the customer. At the same time the value of the services that have to change will be maximized and the number of incidents reduced. Changes in the services come about through this process. Standardized methods and procedures have to be applied. A change is a controlled change to the service assets and configuration items (CIs) within the whole service lifecycle approach.

The Change Manager has final responsibility for this process. Part of these activities involves drawing up, handling, processing and, after approval, (arranging for) building, testing and the implementation of a change. The output of this process is an evaluated and authorized change. Part of making the change itself involves updating the CI data in the Configuration Management Database (CMDB) by the Service Asset and Configuration Management process.

Change Management and Information Security Management

The activities in the Change Management process often show a relationship to security, because security and Change Management are closely linked. If a situation is reached within an acceptable level of security, and this situation is controlled by the change process, the organization can ensure that the new situation has an acceptable level of security as well. A number of fixed steps are distinguished to guarantee this level of security.

Figure 4.7 shows the steps that have to be taken. The input is a Request for Change (RFC) that includes a proposal to change the IT infrastructure or a service, and provides the reasons and the references to the CIs concerned. Parameters are linked to an RFC that trigger the acceptance procedure. The parameters in the figure are intended as an example; other choices are also possible. The choice here is a parameter for the urgency; the reasons for this could be that, without implementation, the SLA could no longer be fulfilled, now or in the near future. An 'impact' parameter is also included, which expresses the impact on the configuration or its management. The 'impact on information security' parameter is also included. If the proposal could have a major impact on information security, more stringent acceptance tests and procedures would be necessary.

Security proposals also form part of the RFC. The starting point is again the agreements contained in the SLA, as well as the basic level of security chosen by the IT service provider. General security profiles are often used to specify which security measures have to be implemented for which types of products. For example, the following have to be specified for each operating system: identification and authentication, authorization, access control, audit/logging, and management (including user management and the management of rights). Security proposals consist of a collection of security measures that are often combined in a procedure laid down in documentation.

The RFC is then assessed and authorized. In the case of a change with limited impact, this can be carried out by the Change Manager or can be delegated. In the case of a change with greater consequences, the decision is taken by the Change Advisory Board (CAB). The CAB always includes the Security Manager, and possibly also the Security Officer of the customer(s), if the change is likely to have a major impact on security.

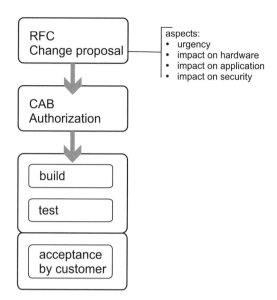

Figure 4.7: Information security in the change process

It is not necessary to involve the Security Manager for every change. As far as possible, security has to be an integrated part of normal tasks. This implies that security has to be in mind whenever changes to specifications occur – for instance, what impact the change may have on security or whether security requirements are needed in addition to the change.

The Change Manager has to be in a position to assess whether a change will have a high impact on security, and whether he/she or the CAB needs input from the Security Manager. The Security Manager is not always required for the selection of measures for the CIs that are involved in the change; if everything is in order, the framework for the measures being taken is ready and the only question is concerned with the way in which they have to be implemented.

In special cases the customer may be represented in the CAB by the Security Officer. The Security Officer is invited by the Change Manager, or the Security Manager.

In implementing the change, the security measures will need to be implemented immediately and then tested. Testing security is different from normal functional testing; normal tests examine whether a particular function is present. When testing security the focus is not only on the presence and efficacy of a (security) function but also on the absence of other unwanted functionality or improper behavior. The functions in the latter category generally account for the gaps in the system.

The Change Advisory Board decides whether or not to accept an RFC. If the CAB approves, the change request is authorized. The CAB's composition will depend on the expertise required to assess an RFC; this is the responsibility of the Change Manager. In the case of a change with a major impact on security, the CAB also includes the Security Manager of the IT service provider.

Depending on the organization and the nature of the changes, the CAB's composition may be as follows:

- Change Manager
- architect
- technical specialist
- developer
- operational manager
- user representatives
- Security Manager.

Finally, the implementation of changes often results in security incidents, with the associated problems that accompany them. Implementing changes on the basis of a plan (that is organizing the changes), will reduce the negative consequences of changes in terms of disruptions.

Change Management in general, and the CAB in particular, have to ensure that the level of security is not reduced by a change, and that it certainly does not fall below the agreed level (the security baseline). This is a point for special attention in the test procedures.

The Operations Manager or CIO (or equivalent role in the organization) is held accountable for the operational IT infrastructure, and hence has a direct interest in ensuring that new developments, patches, fixes and version upgrades etc. will not adversely affect the status quo. The information security and risk management functions can be seen as this role's support, checking whether the change is acceptable or not and, where necessary, slowing down the process until the risks are adequately mitigated. The change proposer, development project manager etc. often have the opposite objectives, to get the change implemented as soon as possible. Dealing diplomatically with such conflicting interests is a key part of the Change Manager's role.

4.3.2 Service Asset and Configuration Management

A prerequisite for effective IT management is that the process for Service Asset and Configuration Management (SACM) is set up properly. The process in ITILv3 has been expanded with all the activities surrounding Service Asset Management. The technical components such as CIs have to be recorded, together with all the other components that make up a service. Service Asset and Configuration Management is the process that ensures that staff know what is available to the organization in terms of services and its IT components, its status, and which relationships exist between the various services and components of the infrastructure (that is, the relationships between the CIs, see below). In short, this process checks whether the inventory of the services as well as the IT infrastructure is known. Service Asset and Configuration Management also ensures that changes in the services and its IT components are only made in an accountable manner. Each change must be recorded in Service Asset and Configuration Management, which forms the basis of IT management.

This process provides control over all the components of the services and IT infrastructure and the related procedures and documentation. It supports the other processes and facilitates management of as well as changes to all these components, within the context of ever-changing user requirements.

When Service Asset and Configuration Management is properly organized, it becomes clear which components make up the services being managed, who is responsible for which component, where the items are, what the status is and what relationship(s) exist between the services.

Service Asset and Configuration Management is responsible for correctly registering authorized parts of the IT infrastructure. Moreover, Service Asset and Configuration Management verifies whether the registration still correctly reflects the situation in reality. This approach avoids having to work with unauthorized components that do not fulfil the security requirements.

There are two central concepts: a Configuration Item (CI) is the smallest unit that is managed individually. The overview of all the CIs also forms the overview of the total IT infrastructure. This overview is called the Service Asset and Configuration Management Database (CMDB). Examples of configuration items in ITIL include software (applications), hardware, documentation and procedures.

Information Security Management and Service Asset and Configuration Management

Each CI has a unique identification number. Records are also kept of each CI's attributes, the status, and the possible relationships to other CIs. In terms of information security, one aspect of Service Asset and Configuration Management that is especially important is the classifying of a CI. The classification links the CI to a particular set of security measures or a procedure.

A CI classification is an indication of the level of confidentiality, integrity and/or availability required for the CI. This classification is derived from the security requirements in the SLA. The customer of the IT service provider (usually a business process owner) determines the classification because he/she is the only person who can determine how important information or systems are for his/her business processes. The customer determines the classification on the basis of an analysis of the dependency of the business processes on the information systems and on the information itself. It is then the IT service provider's responsibility to permanently link this classification to the right CIs. The IT service provider must also implement an individual package of security measures for each level of classification; the package of measures can be summarized in a procedure. Such a procedure may, for example, read: 'procedure for handling data carriers with data classified as private'. It is a good practice for a record to be entered in the SLA about which control objectives or which package of security measures has to be implemented for which level of classification.

Classification of information assets ,or CIs, by confidentiality, integrity and availability is not an end in itself but simply a means of grouping together assets with similar security risks and hence control requirements. In practice, assets near the upper borderline between any classification criteria may well deserve additional controls, or better compliance, than those in the middle or towards the lower borderline. The key to making this work is to allow discretion, ideally 'informed discretion' (i.e. by someone who understands and appreciates the issue). Information Asset Owners are held accountable for adequately protecting their assets, are theoretically empowered to classify their assets and make key decisions about security risks and controls, but in practice they usually need the guidance of risk and security professionals.

A classification system must always be tailored to the needs of the customer's organization. A few examples are provided below.

Confidentiality:
- High   = Personal data as defined under the Data Protection Act (privacy related), medical records, strategic information
- Medium   = Internal, must not go outside the organization
- Low   = External, everything that would be allowed to go outside the organization

Integrity:
- High   = Financial transactions, software, personal data
- Medium   = Measurement data, name and address data
- Low   = No requirements

Availability:
- High   = 24 hours per day, 99.5%
- Medium   = from 07.00 to 19.00, 99%
- Low   = no guarantees required

Other examples of classification schemes are:
- Official: Secret, Confidential, Restricted, Unclassified
- NATO: Cosmic Top Secret, NATO Secret, NATO Confidential, NATO Restricted, NATO Unclassified

Finally, an example from a government department is shown in table 4.2.

Security requirement	Valuation			
	No criterion Security is not really necessary	Advisable A certain degree of security is appreciated	Important Security is absolutely necessary in view of the interests	Essential Security is a primary criterion
Confidentiality	Public The information may be published/ made public	Protected Data only to be seen by particular group	Crucial Data only accessible to those directly involved	Mandatory Business interests would be severely damaged if accessed by unauthorized parties
Integrity	Passive No extra integrity protection required	Active Business process tolerates some errors	Detectable A very small number of errors is permitted	Essential Business process demands error-free information
Availability	Unnecessary No guarantees required	Necessary Occasional downtime is acceptable	Important Hardly any downtime during opening times	Essential Only out of operation in extremely exceptional circumstances

Table 4.2: Example of classification system

These examples show up to four levels of classification for confidentiality, integrity and availability. The more levels a classification system has, the more difficult it is to maintain, so it is advisable to keep the number of levels as low as possible for the service provider's (and its customers') needs.

In the most simple classification system, each security characteristic is designated simply as 'basic level' (to be linked to the set of standard measures of the baseline) or as additional requirements (to be linked to a more stringent set of measures).

An example of a simple classification system is:
• the baseline always applies
• additional requirements apply to confidentiality, if:
  – the information is of a strategic nature
  – the information is specially marked: 'medical', 'private and confidential', 'personal'
• additional requirements apply to integrity and availability, if:
  – the information and the systems are employed for uses of a strategic, mission or safety-critical nature.

To minimize the management overhead, it is advisable to use one classification system, even when an IT service provider has more than one customer.

To summarize: classification is a key concept. The CMDB contains the classification of each CI. The classification links the CI to a set of security measures that relates to the classification, or a procedure. The classification links a CI to specific activities, laid down as a procedure (handling instructions) in the documentation (handbooks, implementation guidelines). The procedure will often state that some type of record or reporting is required on implementation.

4.3.3 Release and Deployment Management
The goal of this process is to implement software version management and to arrange software distribution. The input for this process can be an authorized RFC out of the Change Management process. To this end, this process has what is called the Definitive Media Library. This is the repository of all the correct, recognized, registered, legal and authorized software, possibly with a reference to the source code, the depot and the installation files. This library need not be a separate database; it can just be a part of the CMDB.

Release and Deployment Management and Information Security Management
It is important that all software enters the organization in a controlled manner through this process, which ensures that:
• the correct software is used
• the software is tested in advance
• the introduction is authorized in the correct manner (by means of a change request)
• the software is legal
• the software is imported virus free and remains virus free when distributed
• the version numbers are known (and registered by Configuration Management in the CMDB)
• the latest security patches have been applied and tested
• the vulnerability database has been checked
• the roll-out process is tested in advance

- it is possible to 'back out' and go back to the old situation
- controlled introduction is possible.

This process, too, operates according to a fixed set of procedures, with due attention being paid to information security. It is particularly important for the security implications to be considered during the testing and acceptance stage. This will ensure that the security requirements and measures identified in the SLA will not be compromised.

4.3.4 Service Validation and Testing

The underlying concept to which Service Validation and Testing contributes is quality assurance – establishing that the Service Design and release will deliver a new or changed service or service offering that is fit for purpose and fit for use.

Testing is a vital area within Service Management. If services are not tested to assure that all security requirements are met, then their introduction into the operational environment will bring a rise in incidents, problems, costs and so on. The quality of services is assured through verification and validation, which in turn are delivered through testing.

Testing is related directly to the building of service assets and products so that each one has an associated acceptance test and activity to ensure it meets requirements.

Service Validation and Testing and Information Security Management

Tests are used to provide confidence that the warranties can be delivered. One of the warranties is of course security, which assures that the use of services by customers will be secure. This means that customer assets within the scope of service delivery and support will not be exposed to certain security risks. Service providers undertake to implement general and service level controls that will ensure that the value provided to customers is complete and not eroded by any avoidable costs and risks. In this process it is mentioned that service security covers the following aspects of reducing risks:

- authorized and accountable usage of services as specified by customer
- protection of customers assets from unauthorized or malicious access
- security zones between customer assets and service assets.

Security plays a supporting role to the other three aspects of service warranty and effective security has a positive impact on those aspects. Service security inherits all the general properties of the security of physical and human assets, as well as of that of intangibles such as data, information, coordination and communication.

4.3.5 Knowledge Management

Knowledge Management is focused on maintaining and revealing knowledge and supporting data. Underpinning this knowledge will be a considerable quantity of data, which will be held in a central logical repository or Configuration Management System and CMDB. The Service Knowledge Management System is a broader concept that covers a much wider base of knowledge – for example, the experience of staff, the organization's performance figures, suppliers' and partners' requirements, abilities and expectations.

Knowledge Management and Information Security Management

One of the key points about Knowledge Management is that upfront requirements should be established before data and information is collected. In practice, data is often collected with no clear understanding of how it will be used and this can be costly. For Information Security Management there should be requirements established for:

- data protection, privacy, security, security vulnerability, ownership, agreement restrictions, rights of access, intellectual property and patents with the relevant stakeholder
- defining who needs access to what data and information as well as when they access it, including its relative importance at different times. For example, access to payroll information might be considered more important on the day before the payroll is run than at other times of the month
- procedures such as who may define and publicize rights, obligations and commitments on the retention of, transmission of and access to information and data items, based on applicable requirements and protecting its security, integrity and consistency
- procedures such as who may identify the requirements to review and (if necessary) to adapt, changes in security, service continuity, storage and capacity, especially in the light of new technology.

4.3.6 Evaluation

Evaluation is a generic process that considers whether the performance of something is acceptable, value for money etc. – and whether it will be proceeded with, accepted into use, paid for, etc. The goal of evaluation is to set stakeholder expectations correctly and provide effective and accurate information to Change Management to make sure that changes that adversely affect service capability and introduce risk are not transferred into the operational environment unchecked. The scope of evaluation is limited to the evaluation of new or changed services defined by Service Design, during deployment and before final transition to service operations.

Evaluation and Information Security Management

We would usually expect the intended effects of a change to be beneficial. The unintended effects are harder to predict, often not seen even after the service change is implemented, and frequently ignored. Additionally, they will not always be beneficial, for example in terms of impact on other services, impact on customers and users of the service, and network overloading. Intended effects of a change should match the service acceptance criteria, including the security criteria. Unintended effects are often not seen until the pilot stage or even once in production; they are difficult to measure and very often not beneficial to the business. Risk management should play a major role in assessing the effect of implementing a new or changed service. One of the ways to carry this out is to compare the predicted performance and actual performance. This may involve customer participation. It should be determined that predicted performance and actual performance are acceptable, and that there are no unacceptable risks, otherwise you should draw up a deviations report.

4.3.7 Transition Planning and Support

The goals of Transition Planning and Support are to plan and coordinate the resources to ensure that the requirements of Service Strategy encoded in Service Design are effectively realized in Service Operations and to identify, manage and control the risks of failure and disruption across transition activities. This process supports all the other processes within Service Transition.

Transition Planning and Support and Information Security Management

Transition Planning and Support ensures that Service Transition issues, risks and deviations are reported to the appropriate stakeholders and decision-makers by identifying, managing and controlling the risks of failure and disruption across transition activities.

Questions such as the following should be asked:
• have the risks to the overall services and operations capability been assessed?
• do the people who need to use the service understand and have the requisite skills to use it?
• have potential changes in business circumstances been identified?

4.4   Continual Service Improvement

Continual Service Improvement (CSI) is an ongoing activity that is integral to an organization as opposed to a reactive response to a specific situation or a temporary crisis. Organizations operate in dynamic environments with the need to learn, improve and adapt. CSI provides guidance in maintaining and improving on (better or evolutionary) design, introduction, and operation of services. CSI completes the cycle of the Plan, Do, Check, Act (PDCA) model.

The three main levels of abstraction are:
• the overall 'health' of IT service management
• the continual alignment of the portfolio of IT Services with the current and future business needs
• the maturity of the enabling IT processes required to support business processes in a continual service lifecycle model.

The primary purpose of CSI is to continually (re)align IT services to the changing business needs by identifying and proposing improvements to IT Services that support business processes. These improvement activities support the lifecycle approach through Service Strategy, Service Design, Service Transition and Service Operation. CSI is about looking for ways to improve process effectiveness, efficiency as well as cost effectiveness.

CSI objectives are to:
• review, analyze and make recommendations on improvement opportunities in each lifecycle phase: Service Strategy, Service Design, Service Transition, and Service Operations
• review and analyze service level achievement results, comparing these to SLA targets
• identify and implement individual activities to improve IT service quality and improve the efficiency and effectiveness of enabling management processes
• improve the cost effectiveness of delivering IT services
• ensure applicable quality management methods are used to support continual improvement activities.

Typical examples of CSI activities include the monitoring, assessing and proposing of improvements of:
• organizational and process change and management
• implementation of roles, responsibilities and ownership

- execution of key-activities such as risk management
- functioning of processes and compliance with external/internal agreements
- the ongoing process to align with internal and external business drivers
- patch levels, hardening and adherence to technical standards (settings)
- service level management.

CSI support for Information Security Management
Focusing on Information Security Management, CSI support for Information Security Management may consist of:
- compliance with baselines
- compliance with additional service specific regulation
- ongoing risk management
- providing assurance and reporting on risk and security to customers.

Many of the CSI objectives focus on completing the PDCA cycle. CSI processes and activities can contribute to Information Security Management in many ways, most notably:
- the seven-step improvement process
  - includes improvement on risk and security
  - defining metrics and measurement for Information Security Management
- service reporting
  - reporting on achievements and performance on risk and Information Security Management
  - reporting on conformity with policy, rules and SLAs
  - providing assurance to the market and customers
- service measurement
  - metrics/KPIs for security
  - policy monitoring (hardening)
  - audit and compliance monitoring
  - benchmarking
- service level management
  - compliance with SLAs
  - compliance with internal policies
  - compliance with baselines
  - a security improvement program.

These topics are further explored in the following subsections.

4.4.1   The seven-step improvement process

Figure 4.8: Seven-step improvement process

Figure 4.8 sketches the seven-step improvement process from CSI. This improvement process is a 'measure and feedback'-cycle on the current service provisioning. The principle of this improvement process is that goals are translated to activities, whose effectiveness and performance are measured.

The seven-step improvement process for information risk and Information Security Management

The seven-step improvement process is a general process that can also be applied to Information Security Management. The seven-step improvement process reads as follows.

1. Define what you should measure
- Translate the goals (typically these are the control objectives or risks) to controls. Note that controls include activities and measures.
- The maturity level also gives a key to what you should measure:
  - In the Ad Hoc phase, backup and incident management are key
  - In the Controlled phase, the effective implementation of the baseline is to be measured. An accepted practice to be used as baseline is the Code of Practice for Information Security Management (ISO/IEC 27002). This would normally imply the assessment of effectiveness of implementation of the control from this standard. Key controls are:
    - hardening of components, patch management
    - authorization and access management
    - management of incidents, events, alarms, etc.
    - control of operation
    - control of Change Management

- In the service oriented phase, in addition the service-oriented risk management should be measured. Typically this would include:
    - identification of the most relevant services
    - risk analysis performed per service or per group of services
    - management of risks (risk removal, mitigation, transfer, acceptance)
- In the customer oriented phase, in addition to the previous phases the following is measured:
    - the performance of customer-oriented risk management
    - customer specific compliance reporting and assurance
- Finally in the business oriented phase, the following activities are measured:
    - execution and reporting and business-specific compliance programs
    - periodic alignment with stakeholders, such as oversight bodies.
- Note that the required rigor/depth ('certainty') of the assurance varies depending on the target users of the provided assurance. Within a service provider's organization a unified assurance process is advised; however, differentiation on reporting should ensure that the specific customer's requirements are reflected, taking into account the maturity of the customer as well.

2. Define what you can measure
- Make a list of the key activities and measures that support the achievement of the goals identified above.
- Define which output and/or reporting from security and risk controls is expected and when.
- Define, e.g. by means of a RACI matrix (R = Responsible, A = Accountable, C = Consulted, I = Informed), what is to be expected from whom.
- Define an assurance program with:
    - supervision
    - internal control
    - self-assessments and peer reviews
    - internal audit
    - external audit
    - certification
    - third party assurance such as SAS-70 or ISAE 3402.

3. Gathering the data
- Note that data can be gathered from people, processes and technology by automated tools.

4. Processing the data

5. Analyzing the data
- The central question is 'did we meet the objectives?'

6. Presenting and using the information
- Use the result in defining Security Improvement Plans
    - improvement of activities/in processes
    - improvement of controls, measures
    - improvement of policies, rules, regulations, etc
    - improvement of information risk management, assurance processes and tooling

- Assurance reporting includes:
  - internal reporting
  - generic reporting for all customers
  - specific reporting to individual customers
  - certificates and/or third party confirmation.

7. Implementing corrective action
- Implement the Security Improvement Program

Note that metrics on baseline security are included in the ISO/IEC 27004 – Metrics and Measurement for Information Security Management.

4.4.2 Service Reporting
The Service Reporting process includes reporting on (the management of) risks and security.

Service Reporting support for Information Security Management
A good practice is to match the reporting to the maturity levels of the target audience:
- ad hoc phase: reporting on incidents
- controlled phase: reporting on compliance with the baseline.
  - KPIs or key controls may be identified. See above for a typical list of key controls
- service oriented phase: generic reports on service oriented risk control
- customer oriented phase: compliance reporting is specific and tailored to the customer. Reporting on customer-specific risk management is included as well
- business oriented phase: reporting, possibly to an oversight body, in externally defined formats.

In addition, it is recommended good practice to report on the progress of the Security Improvement Program as well as reporting on special events and developments relevant to the target audience.

Note that the security measurement process is needed to collect reportable data. The operational effectiveness of this process determines the 'certainty' that is reflected in the reporting and should therefore be reported on as well. In this way, the users of the reports are able to assess whether or not these reports provide sufficient assurance, or whether additional assurance strengthening is needed, e.g. through certification, external audits or third party confirmation.

Frameworks, models, standards for Information Security Management systems
In Service Strategy the applicable standards for reference or implementation are chosen. Many standards exist, and most of them are comparable. In Annex A, a comparison is provided between widely used standards for the Controlled-phase. For customers, reference to a standard that they know helps to establish trust and avoid confusion. Service providers focus on multi-compliancy frameworks, where the internal control framework provides assurance for a small number of standards that are in use by their customers. The standards usually describe process requirements and/or controls (measures and activities).

Industry accepted standards for Information Security Management by maturity level are:
- ad hoc: no standards
- controlled: ISO/IEC 27000-series and COBIT
- service oriented risk management: M_o_R, Sprint/IRAM, CRAMM
- customer oriented: specific standards
- business oriented: many standards exist, e.g. from financial institutions oversight bodies, Payment Card Industry standards, etc.

4.4.3 Service Measurement

The goal of Service Measurement is to measure the performance of a service via predefined parameters or KPIs. These KPIs are defined in the design process. The values of the KPIs or the ranges of their values are typically reflected in the SLAs between customer and service provider; these KPIs are the basis for the periodic service reports. When certain thresholds are exceeded, escalation takes place.

Service Measurement support for Information Security Management: security measuring

Security measurement is defined based on the seven-step improvement process, applied for security (see 4.4.1). Sometimes a balanced scorecard for security is used. There are several ways in which security can be measured.

Measuring technical security can be done by:
- measuring compliance with patch levels/hardening standards (traffic light reporting denotes where these levels are current)
- measuring the number of events detected/attacks prevented (as a percentage of the average)
- measuring the number of incidents (as a percentage of the average number of incidents).

For housing and hosting, automated tools exist for vulnerability maintenance, automated patch management, intrusion detection and prevention, policy monitoring (checking the settings of systems on a regular basis), security incident and event management, etc. These automated tools are combined and maintained in a Security Operating Center. Often the support of a Computer Emergency Response Team (CERT) can help you to monitor and assess the impact of new threats and vulnerabilities for your organization.

Other parts of the baseline can be measured by a combination of supervision, (controlled) self-assessments, internal audits and other assurance means. Traffic light reporting may be used.

The security improvement plan is developed in the following steps:
- business impact analysis/risk analysis is performed (percentage of critical services)
- a risk treatment plan is defined: identified risks are accepted, mitigated, transferred or a security improvement plan is accepted (percentage of critical services)
- monitoring the progress of the security improvement plan (percentage of progress or 'traffic light' reporting).

In the customer-oriented phase, the measurement is customer-specific. It is a good practice to define a dashboard for compliance monitoring that is based on a risk analysis between the service provider and the customer. This risk analysis should be performed on a regular basis.

Measuring should, where possible, be on results (output) and not on effort.

4.4.4 Service Level Management

The main objective of Service Level Management is to deliver a service with the quality as agreed in the SLAs. Service level management is both externally oriented (reporting to the customers about achievements and the provided value), and internally oriented (organizing the internal processes such that agreements are met).

Security Service Level Management

Service Level Management for Security is similar to other types of Service Level Management. Where SLAs are generally described in terms of the desired functionality; information security has also to do with the absence of leaks, flaws, etc, the control of risks (controlling likelihood and impact of incidents) and the management of controls.

Information Security Management reports, as any other process, via Service Level Management to the customers. Emergency communication lines should be established upfront but only be used in case of (severe) incidents and disasters. A good practice is to have the possibility of direct communication between the customer's Information Security Officer, Privacy Officer and/or Business Continuity Manager with their counterparts within the service provider.

Normal processes to be established between the customer and service provider for Information Security Management include incident management, authorization/access management and continuity management.

Internally, the Information Security Management process, either directly or via Service Level Management, has to organize and coordinate all risk and security related activities within other processes. Information Security Management is a tactical process, so it has only a limited number of activities within the process itself. Most activities are coordinated through Information Security Management, but are executed in other processes, e.g. in Service Operation.

Building and maintaining relationships is key. CSI support for Information Security Management may include the requirement for CSI to assess and verify that all responsible functions within the organization implement these responsibilities and report honestly and openly. The results of this assessment can be used for the Security Improvement and maintenance Program.

4.4.5 Continual Service Improvement (CSI) methods and tools

CSI can make use of methods and tools in support of the Information Security Management process. Some are procedural, others make use of technical tools. Some examples follow in this subsection.

CSI methods and tools to support Information Security Management
The most common methods and tools for Information Security Management are:
- control frameworks
- authority matrices
- assessments of controls
- tools to support the IT operation.

Control frameworks
Risk Management (see 'Service Strategy support for Information Security Management') together with applicable rules and regulations, helps to define control objectives. These objectives are implemented by one or more controls, for which responsibilities are allocated in the organization. These controls are usually laid down in the organization's control framework(s); it is not uncommon to have different control frameworks for legal, technical and organizational/process compliance.

Authority matrices
An easy way to define responsibilities is the use of RACI matrices, where
- R: Responsible – the function or person responsible for implementing the control and reporting on effectiveness
- A: Accountable – only one (1) person is accountable
- C: Consulted – involvement of other functions
- I: Informed – receiving reports on the results

Assessment of controls
For the whole control framework, assessments should be defined. The effectiveness of some controls may need to be checked daily, whereas other controls may only need to be checked once a year. Where direct assessment is needed, the proper instrument is supervision. If sampling on, say, a daily or monthly basis is sufficient, management or internal control can be used. Note that these types of control assessment are typically used by management. To support senior management, internal or external audits can be used. Audits are typically done at most once a year. Note that 'supervision' gives the most direct checking; external audit necessarily only makes a very superficial inspection of the organization and the set of controls. It is all a matter of balance, and the different ways of assessing controls should build upon each other.

The message here is that 'closing the loop' of the PDCA cycle is essential to maintain an effective control framework. So, checking effective implementation of controls is of great value to the service provider organization and its customers.

Instruments for control assessment and assurance
The following instruments have already been mentioned:
- supervision
- internal control
- internal and external audits.

In addition, the following instruments may be beneficial in providing assurance:

- balanced scorecard for security: defining the KPIs for security and the external reporting about these KPIs. Note that balanced scorecard reporting can be done by the service provider, to support the assurance needs of many customers
- benchmarking: comparing the services of different organizations. Typically benchmarking focuses on KPIs for security, including uptime, incidents, security baseline, helpdesk. Benchmarking is performed by a third party, making use of the results provided by the organizations participating in the benchmark
- certification: the organization (customer or service provider) can obtain security certification with a small number of industry standards. The most widely used is the ISO/IEC 27001 certificate, based on the Code of Practice for Information Security Management. Certification is done by independent (lead) assessors from certification bodies, with oversight from accreditation organizations
- third party assessments: within each country different types of third party assessments exist. Internationally, the SAS-70 and the ISAE 3402 are recognized assurance standards. Third party assessments are always done by independent external parties.

Technical tools

These include tools that support and protect the integrity of the network, systems and applications, guarding against intrusion and inappropriate access and usage. As in the Systems and Network Management domain, all Security-related hardware and software solutions should generate alerts that will trigger the auto-generation of incidents for management through the normal processes.

There are many Information Security Management suites and technical tools. Some examples are:

- hardening/vulnerability management: some tools monitor on an ongoing basis the parameter settings, patch levels and other security related information on the level of the platforms and sometimes also of the more popular applications. Input on newly detected vulnerabilities, as available from sources such as the SANS and FIRST community, may be used to assess their impact on the organization. Security policy monitoring should be done at regular intervals by the organization's internal policy owners and changes can be enforced. Reporting on detected vulnerabilities takes place centrally
- intrusion detection and prevention: when hacking attempts, from outside or from within the organization, take place, these tools should detect any intrusion and react to it. Their naming varies from Intrusion Detection and Prevention to Security Incident and Event Management
- automated incident and event management
- logging, monitoring and alerting: either to detect identified events directly, or be able to look back at the history of events.

Sometimes the management of and reporting of these tools is centralized in a Security Operating Centre.

Tools for security testing

Another set of tools supports the security testing of new information systems. These tools are referred to as Test Support Tool Sets, and include among many others stress testing, assessment of robustness of input validation, penetration testing and security scans.

4.5 Service Operation

Service Operation is the phase in the Information Security Management lifecycle that is responsible for 'business-as-usual' activities. Strategic objectives are ultimately realized through Service Operations, therefore making it a critical capability. Service Operation is the 'factory' of IT, which implies a closer focus on the day-to-day activities and infrastructure that are used to deliver services. In many ways security aspects are involved in these day-to-day activities.

The purpose of Service Operation is to coordinate and carry out the activities and processes required to deliver and manage services at agreed levels to business users and customers. Service Operation is also responsible for the ongoing management of the technology that is used to deliver and support services.

The scope of Service Operation includes the services themselves, the Service Management processes, technology and people. All services require some form of technology to deliver them. Managing this technology (or security technology) is not a separate issue, but an integral part of the management of the services. The impact of proper behavior of employees should not be underestimated. Ultimately, your staff manages the technology, processes and services.

Service Operation in ITIL version 3 is neither an organizational unit nor a single process, but it does include several functions and many processes and activities. Within the core book Service Operations the following processes are dealt with:
- Event Management
- Request Fulfilment
- Incident Management
- Problem Management
- Access Management.

In addition there are four functions:
- Service Desk
- application management
- technical management
- IT Operations.

4.5.1 Event Management
An event can be defined as any detectable or discernible occurrence that has significance for the management of the IT Infrastructure or the delivery of IT service and evaluation of the impact a deviation might cause to the services. Events are typically notifications created by an IT service, Configuration Item (CI) or monitoring tool.

Event Management is the process that detects and monitors all events that occur through the IT infrastructure to allow for normal operation and also to detect and escalate exception conditions.

There are three types of events: informational, warning and exception.

Informational

This refers to an event that does not require any action and does not represent an exception. They are typically stored in the system or service log files and kept for a predetermined period. Informational events are typically used to check on the status of a device or service, or to confirm the successful completion of an activity.

Examples of informational events include a user logging on to an application, a job in the batch queue completes successfully, a device has come online, a transaction is completed successfully.

Warning

A warning is an event that is generated when a service or device is approaching a threshold. Warnings are intended to notify the appropriate person, process or tool so that the situation can be checked and the appropriate action taken to prevent an exception. Examples of warnings are: memory use on a server is currently at 65% and increasing. If it reaches 75%, response times will be unacceptably long or the collision rate on a network has increased by 15% over the past hour.

Exception

An exception means that a service or device is currently operating abnormally (however this may be defined). Typically, this means that an SLA has been breached and the business is being affected. Exceptions could represent a total failure, impaired functionality or degraded performance. Be aware, however, that an exception does not always represent an incident. For example, an exception could be generated when an unauthorized device is discovered on the network. Examples of exceptions include: a server is down, response time of a standard transaction across the network has slowed to more than 15 seconds, more than 150 users have logged on to the critical application concurrently, etc.

Event Management and Information Security Management

Events may occur in different forms and formats. The important point is that the business should be informed whenever there appears to be a security breach on business applications and/or business processes, to allow potentially significant security events to be detected and acted upon (e.g. a business application reports abnormal activity on a customer's account that may indicate some sort of fraud or security breach).

Incidents should be analysed internally by information security experts and others, before deciding that customers or to be notified. This should be a standard part of the incident management and escalation process. This communication process preferably goes via Service Management and may involve use of a corporate communication department.

One of the most important critical success factors is achieving the correct level of filtering. This is complicated by the fact that the significance of events changes. For example, a user logging into a system today is normal, but if that user leaves the organization and subsequently tries to log on, it is a security breach. In another example a user tries several times to log in into a application. What does this signify? The user may have forgotten their password after a long vacation or sickness leave and the event has nothing to do with security. Without contextual information it is difficult to determine whether the event is a security breach or not.

4.5.2 Request Fulfilment

Request Fulfilment is the processes of dealing with Service Requests from the users. The term 'Service Request' is used as a generic description for many varying types of demands that are placed upon the IT department by the users. Often these standard requests are for a reset of a password or a request to install a certain application. Some organizations that have to deal with large numbers of standard requests let them be handled by Change Management. In other organizations they are handled by the Incident Management process. The reason why in ITIL v3 there is a separate process for Request Fulfilment is not to obstruct or congest the normal Incident Management or Change Management processes.

A 'quick win' is to decide within the Design phase which service requests are standard, how they are going to be handled and who is going to approve them (e.g. financial approvals).

Request Fulfilment offers good opportunities for self-help practices where users can generate a Service Request using technology that links into Service Management tools. Ideally, users should be offered a 'menu' type of selection via a web interface, so that they can select and input details of Service Requests from a predefined list.

Request Fulfilment and Information Security Management

Security policies will prescribe any controls to be executed or adhered to when providing the service – for example, ensuring that the requester is authorized to access the service, or that the software is licensed.

One of the risks involved is that standard service requests such as resetting a password may be handled in a standard way without questioning authenticity or confidentiality. Adequate security monitoring capabilities would be useful in that type of situation. In general, there should be agreement within the security policy that makes it clear who may and may not make a standard request.

4.5.3 Incident Management

Providing continuity for the user is the most important goal of Incident Management. The user has to be able to carry on working: if the user is satisfied with the solution, the incident can be closed from the ITIL point of view, even if the solution is simply 'press reset'. This process is concerned with minimising interruption of service to the user, and not with solving underlying problems in the IT infrastructure (which is the domain of Problem Management).

The activities of the Incident Management process are the administration, monitoring and management of incidents (incident control). The Service Desk is the function or central point where all incidents are registered and monitored; it acts as a single source of help for all incident reports and first-line help and is the 'owner' of all the incidents.

Within this process incidents are recorded and the aim is to ensure that they are dealt with as quickly as possible.

Incidents are categorized and for each category a procedure is defined that prescribes the activities that have to be carried out, mostly by the Service Desk. Accurate categorization is essential for security (see below). An indication of the effect (impact) of an incident is often used. If the impact directly jeopardizes the fulfilment of the SLA, it will have a higher priority than incidents for which a workaround exists. When an incident is registered, a link is made as quickly as possible to the service affected by the incident. An incident number or ticket is issued for the incident, which is provided to the incident reporter, in case he/she wishes to make any additional reports about the incident or wants a follow-up on its resolution. If possible, the reporter is helped immediately, possibly with a temporary solution.

The output consists of immediate solutions or alternative ways of working. Incidents are registered in every case and these records form the input for the Problem Management process.

Incident Management and Information Security Management

The Service Desk is the main liaison point for security incidents. In a procedural sense, security incidents are no different from any other incidents to the Service Desk: the incidents are registered and the proper procedure for dealing with them is selected (the categorization of the incident). In the case of security incidents, depending on the incident's seriousness, a different procedure from that for normal incidents may apply. It is essential for the Service Desk to recognize a security incident as such. Security incidents, in any case, include all those incidents that may impede the fulfilment of the security requirements in the SLA. It is helpful if the SLA includes a summary of the types of incidents that have to be considered as security incidents, which would include those incidents that impede the achievement of the organization's own basic level of security (baseline). The baseline is the level adopted by the IT organization for its own security and from the viewpoint of good housekeeping or 'due diligence' for the customers.

Some typical examples of security incidents include:
- possible breaches of confidentiality requirements:
  - incidents that made unauthorized access to information possible
  - loss of data stores off the premises
  - loss or theft of a laptop, USB-stick or other media
  - attempts to acquire higher authorization by the organization's own staff
  - attempts from inside or outside to gain access to systems (hacking)
- possible breaches of integrity requirements:
  - loss of data or incomplete processing of transactions
  - viruses, Trojan horses (malicious software)
  - bad tracks on hard disks, parity errors in the memory
  - faulty checksums or hash values
- possible breaches of availability requirements:
  - interruption of the service for an unacceptable period. If the interruption lasts longer than a period agreed in the SLA and cannot be rectified within a certain period, the contingency plan comes into effect. (This topic is dealt with under the Contingency Planning process)
  - viruses, Trojan horses (malicious software)
  - theft of laptops, components or data carriers.

Note that the reporting of security incidents will not always stem from users or IT personnel, but also from management, on the basis of alarm reports or audit data from the systems, for example. Note also that (for example) theft of a laptop is initially a breach of availability, but there are now potential breaches of confidentiality (disclosure of data held on the laptop) and integrity (data on the laptop is modified or deleted or is virus infected). So the list of potential impacts of a single incident can become more complex.

The handling of security incidents

Several considerations may apply only to a security incident, which makes it important to think about a different resolution of security incidents.

Legal issues, crime

If a security incident is caused by deliberate intent then in some cases there could be a possible case of a crime. To be able to file for damages and give evidence in court, the evidence that is gathered should be sound also in a legal sense. Normal incident recording might not be adequate for a court hearing.

Some insight in relevant legislation is needed. A security incident may affect the loss of privacy-relevant data. Reporting of such incidents is in some countries mandatory. In addition, the computer crime and abuse acts should be mentioned which, depending on applicable law, may involve reporting certain offenses. These legal specifics should form an integral part of the control framework.

Broad incident analysis

Often a security incident could have an impact that is not confined to the service or IT system where the incident was originally detected. For example, a virus on a mail system has spread to mission-critical systems. In normal incident handling the highest priority is to continue the service as quickly as possible, but with a security incident the impetus is more on restricting unnecessary damage and restricting knowledge about the incident.

Estimating damage done

With the analysis of a security incident, even more business impacts have to be taken into account than with normal incident handling. For instance there might need to be an estimate of the damage to the corporate reputation or information if reliability has been compromised.

Restricting unnecessary damage

In security incident handling there is a far greater chance than with normal incident handling that the wrong approach could create more unnecessary damage or even lose evidence. Consider that an attacker, from within or outside your company, may have anticipated normal handling procedures.

Restricting the knowledge of a security incident

Some organizations consider it wise to restrict knowledge of the security incident, and to keep it confined to a small group of people (so as not to raise unnecessary panic). Information about security incidents is treated as more confidential than information about normal incidents.

Security vulnerabilities of an IT service may require shutting down the service until the vulnerabilities are fixed. They should be handled with particular care because a leak of information to the outside world could cause an immediate attack on the service.

All in all, the management of security incidents could be treated as a separate process, further divided into three general activities: preparation, handling and evaluation (see figure 4.9).

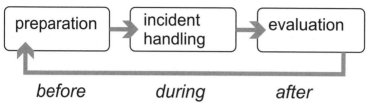

Figure 4.9: Security incident handling

Preparation
This activity should guarantee that an organization can respond adequately to security incidents. For instance, this might include setting up a Computer Emergency Response Team specifically to handle security incidents, security behavior guidelines for personnel for how to react, a newsletter, awareness campaigns, setting up a security incident response plan, education, etc.

Resolution
The security incident response plan should deal with identifying the cause and impact of the incident, to restrict the expansion of the damage, to eliminate vulnerabilities and restore service(s).

Evaluation
This activity should enforce that the whole Plan-Do-Check-Act cycle is being done. A management report should encompass a damage analysis, to learn from the past, to improve the incident response plan or other procedures and to help to prevent similar incidents in the future.

It can be seen from the above that it is essential for the Service Desk to recognize a security incident as such. A formal but impractical definition of security incident is: each incident that may impede the fulfilment of the security requirements in the SLA. In practice it is sufficient if the SLA includes a summary of the (say) ten types of incident that have to be considered as security incidents. Security incidents are also those incidents that impede the achievement of the organization's own basic level of security (baseline). The baseline is the level adopted by the IT service provider to offer a common level of security for all its customers, and to meet its own security requirements.

The categorization of security incidents
It might occur that a security incident has to be treated as confidential in order to minimize the consequential losses, or to create better opportunities for discovering the cause of the security incident (but this must never be an excuse for not reporting a security incident!). It is therefore worthwhile considering classifying security incidents as well. It is always advisable to agree on a procedure for the communication about security incidents, because this would not be for the first time that an organization panics because of an exaggerated rumor. Nor would it be the first time that unnecessary losses were incurred because a security incident was reported too late. It is advisable for all the communication concerned with security incidents to take place via the security manager.

Describing the nature of a security incident is necessary but not in itself sufficient. There also has to be a certain level of security awareness among employees. This is dealt with in more detail in paragraph 5.2.

Security incident control

The handling of security incidents is important. Despite all efforts of devising and implementing measures, security incidents will happen – whether it is the 'simple' disappearance of a mail shipment with crucial information, the third crash in a row of a batch job, a fire at a neighbour's premises or a 'bad news' story on the Internet about the very platform your organization is using.

It might not always be clear whether an incident really is a security incident. However, there is one general rule for dealing with all uncertainty: when in doubt, treat it as a security incident.

Information security will only work if security incidents are processed in an orderly manner. Part of handling a security incident is to solve it by correcting whatever has to be corrected; another part is initiating actions to prevent reoccurrence. Depending on the damage that stems from the security incident, this may involve introducing new security measures. It might also mean that sanctions are put in place to prevent repetition.

Every organizational unit should have a point where security incidents can be reported (usually the Service Desk). At the same time, people should be informed of the possibility of using a point of contact one level up. The reason for this is that even security liaison points or managers have been known to cause security incidents.

It may even be considered appropriate to accept reports of security incidents anonymously. The report's submission has greater priority than persuading the reporter to give their name. Anonymity should, however, be an exception. Security incident reporting is part of the learning process: staff is to be applauded for reporting security incidents.

The reporting process helps to determine where improvements in security are possible or required. Reporting incidents should not be something to be afraid of, but something employees do because it is normal and good for the business.
A procedure for security incident reporting that includes using a predefined form should be described in the security handbook. It will help ensure that important information is not forgotten and that the information is submitted through the right channels.

Escalation is required as soon as the point occurs when solving the security incident exceeds the authority of the organizational unit. For instance, shutting down the network might have serious consequences for other parts of the organization, or even for third parties. In order to escalate, it must be very clear that escalation is in order. The same simple decision tree as that used for problem solving is required, for example, whenever a security incident involves more than the individual organizational unit, or whenever a given period for solving the problem has passed. These rules have to be included in the security incident handling procedure and use of this procedure must be ensured.

Security incident registration

In security incident handling, incident registration is important enough to be dealt with separately. The best stepping stone for implementing information security is a history of mishaps. Unfortunately, beginners in the security domain never have an accurate picture of the things that did not work in the past. There may be logs, but extracting trends from them is almost impossible.

Security incidents will be registered as part of incident reporting (also see the Service Desk function). This involves recording and keeping at least the following data:
- date, time, report serial number, CIs
- date, time of security incident
- details of the reporter (optional; anonymous reports will be accepted)
- descriptive title
- detailed description
- estimate of damage (if appropriate)
- urgency
- organizational unit where the security incident occurred or was noticed
- system or infrastructure affected
- point of contact to ask questions/report result
- escalation status
- solution.

Having a history of security incidents will enable an analysis of the effectiveness of measures, of the seriousness of the things that can go wrong, and of the trends, etc. It will prove a valuable Information Security Management instrument for Problem Management.

4.5.4 Problem Management

Problem Management aims to find the underlying causes of incidents; sometimes finding the links between incidents reveals the root cause. This can be followed by measures to prevent the incidents from reoccurring. This approach also makes it possible to detect security 'leaks'. The Problem Management process is intended to manage, establish links and systematically solve the causes of the security incidents and other incidents, and then to eliminate those causes. If the cause of a problem is determined, a known error can be defined.

The output of the Problem Management process consists of known errors, and Requests for Change (RFCs). An RFC is a proposal for a change in the IT infrastructure. The solutions are carefully documented and made accessible to the Service desk under keywords. The known errors and the RFCs provide the input for the Change Management process.

Problem Management and Information Security Management

If the status of one or a collection of security incidents changes into a problem, it may be that a separate procedure has to be followed. A number of issues are particularly important:
- first and foremost, consider the people who may be involved or who may know something about the security incident(s). This is because it is advisable to keep the group of people who know about security incidents as small as possible (loss of face, good reputation). Knowledge of a possible security leak should also be kept to the minimum to prevent the possibility of the knowledge being misused or the leak being exploited

- secondly, consider the people who are essential to involve in finding a solution for the security incidents (the security manager of the IT service provider, and possibly the customer's security officer)
- the third test in preparing for a solution is to always ensure that no new security issues arise on account of the solution (test in terms of the fulfilment of the SLA and the organization's own security policy and baseline).

4.5.5 Access Management

The operational process Access Management is new in ITIL version 3, which gives authorized users the right to use a particular IT service or group of services that are documented in the Service Catalog and denies or prevents that right to others. Within some organizations it is called Rights Management or Identity Management. In brief, it is the execution of policies and actions defined in Security Management and Availability Management.

Access refers to the level and extent of a service's functionality or data that a user is entitled to use. *Identity* refers to the information that distinguishes a user as an individual and which verifies his/her status within the organization. By definition, the identity of a user is unique to that user within the organization. **Rights** (sometimes called privileges) refer to the actual settings whereby a user is provided access to a service or group of services. Typical rights, or levels of access include read, write, append, execute, change, delete.

Access Management is composed of the following activities.

Requesting access
This is triggered by an RFC, service request or a manager who decides that someone may use a service or a group of services. This request should originate from an authoritative source in the customer's organization.

Verification
Every request to access a service should be verified from two perspectives:
- is the user who asks for access indeed the person who they say they are?
- has the user a legitimate reason to use the service?

The first category is usually achieved by the user providing their username and password. The second category will require some independent verification, other than the user's request. For example, you may need notification from Human Resources that the person is a new employee and requires both a username and access to a standard set of services or authorization from an appropriate manager (as defined in the process).

Providing rights
Access Management merely executes the policies and regulations defined during Service Strategy and Service Design. Access Management enforces decisions to restrict or provide access, rather than making the decision. The more roles and groups that exist, the more likely that role conflict will arise. Role conflict in this context refers to a situation where two specific roles or groups, if assigned to a single user, will create issues with separation of duties or conflict of interest. Examples of this include one role that requires detailed access, while another role prevents that access or

two roles allow a user to perform two tasks that should not be combined (e.g. a contractor can log their time sheet for a project and then approve all payment on work for the same project).

Role conflict can be avoided by careful creation of roles and groups, documenting them and escalating to the stakeholders to resolve.

Monitoring identity status

The roles people play may change over time and so may their demands for a service or group of services. Access Management tools should provide features that enable a user to be moved from one state to another, or from one group to another, easily and with an audit trail. There should also be periodic checks of access rights in force and whether the access gained was used appropriately.

Logging and tracking access

Access Management should react to requests for access and actively monitor the application and technical rights to check that the rights that have been provided are properly used.

Most systems should log successful logins and failed login attempts; this should normally be a baseline control. Some systems should log logouts too, and additional logging of or alerting on use of access rights (particularly privileged access and use of sensitive system functions, including anything to do with setting/resetting security or audit parameters) is a matter of risk mitigation and should be part of the design of the specific system.

Logging/alerting on all these things is ineffective unless the logs/alerts are monitored, analysed and followed up by someone, ideally in real-time but. if not, periodically (depending again on the risk of failing to identify possible abuse of the system in good time). This is a key area where automated tools can help reduce the tedium and increase the effectiveness of control.

Removing or restricting access or rights

Access Management is also responsible for revoking those rights. There needs to be an explicit link between the security administration function and the Human Resources (HR) discipline so that changes in a person's employment status is reflected promptly in changes to their access rights. The process must equally cater for external contractors and consultants who may not be handled by HR. Furthermore, the periodic review of access rights, plus automated suspension of unused access rights after a defined period (where justified by the risks), act as back-stops in case this process fails. This should be governed by the security policies set from the start.

Access Management and Information Security Management

Access Management executes the security policies that were set out in the Design phase of a service. Information Security Management is a key driver for Access Management as it will provide the security and data protection policies and tools needed to execute Access Management. Request Fulfilment (or Change/Incident Management) also plays a major role as standard access can be considered a standard service request. Access Management should also be tightly linked to the Human Resources (HR) department to verify the user's identity as well as to ensure that users are entitled to the services being requested.

The identity of a user is unique to that user within the organization. This may look like a simple concept but from a security point of view the real identity of a user may be hard to establish. There are cases where users may share the same information (e.g. they have the same surname) or the information of a user may be hacked (identity theft). It is wise to establish the identity of a user by using several data types like biometric information (e.g.. fingerprints, retinal images, voice recognition) and physical information (e.g.. passport, driver's license, birth certificate, etc) besides the more common information such as name and address. Most organizations will verify a user's identity before they join the organization by requesting a subset of the above information. The more secure the organization, the more types of information are required and the more thoroughly these are checked. Within the field of service management the hard way is to monitor the access and rights already given; many organizations still fail to have proper exit procedures. Well-defined procedures between IT and HR/Contracting should be established that include failsafe checks that ensure accounts are blocked and access rights are removed immediately when they are no longer justified or required.

Users may have more than one account name. This is a burden to validate implementation of separation of duties. There is also the possibility of users sharing their passwords with colleagues – that is, group accounts (whether sanctioned by management or not). A key control is to hold a single nominal owner personally accountable for each and every computer account, so even if the account is used by members of a team, the team leader is personally liable if they abuse their access.

4.5.6 Service Desk
The Service Desk is a single liaison point of contact within the organization for end-users of services. This functional group is often referred to as a Service Desk. Its core process is normally incident management. The main objective of this function is continuity in the service provided to the customers. This also means that users have to accept the Service Desk as the only source of help, which requires good access to the Service Desk. The Service Desk also has the possibility of escalation, if there is a likelihood of an incident not being solved in good time, which naturally also applies to incidents that concern security. The Service Desk's input largely consists of reports from users.

It is essential for the Service Desk to recognize a security incident as such. Only then will it be possible to set in motion the correct procedure for dealing with security incidents. If the security incident concerns a service or a CI with a higher classification, it may be possible to follow a different procedure, for example. It may be necessary for the IT service provider's security manager to notify the customer's security officer. The customer's security officers serve as the points of contact between the customer and the provider in connection with security. Other follow-up activities may also be defined in the procedure, including reports to the customer. The problem is therefore concerned with how the Service Desk recognizes a security incident. It is advisable to include examples of security incidents in the SLA; it is also advisable to lay down the procedure for various types of security incidents in the SLA.

4.5.7 Service Operation functions

In ITIL v3 four functions are described: Service Desk, Application Management, IT Operations and Technical Management. The last three contain a number of operational activities that ensure that technology is aligned with the overall service and process objectives. These activities are sets of specialized technical activities, all aimed at ensuring that the technology required to deliver and support services is operating effectively and efficiently. These technical activities will vary depending on the type of services being delivered. These activities are not about managing the technology for the sake of having good technology performance; they are about achieving performance that will integrate the technology component with the people and process components to achieve service and business objectives.

All four functions are needed for a stable IT Operations [CAZ] environment (see figure 4.10). They are logical functions, which means that (for instance) Technical Management and Application Management can be executed by one or several departments.

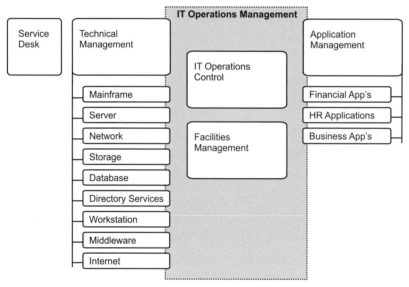

Figure 4.10: Service Operations functions

The figure shows an overview of all the Service Operation functions:
- the Service Desk
- Technical Management, which is a group of IT staff with specialist knowledge and experience about a certain operating system, network, database system and so on. These people play a significant part in supporting, designing, testing, implementing and improving IT services in their own field of expertise
- Application Management, which is responsible for the management of applications during their lifecycle. Application Management plays a daily role in the support, design, testing, implementing and improving applications that are a component of the IT services

- IT Operations, which has two unique functions:
  - IT Operations Control, in which operators take care of day-by-day routine monitoring activities; activities grouped together are sometimes called 'Operations Bridge' or 'Network Operations Center'
  - Facilities Management, which reflects the management of physical IT environment like a data center.

Service Operation and Information Security Management

Information Security Management has overall responsibility for setting policies, standards and procedures to ensure the protection of the organization's assets, data, information and IT services. Service Operation teams cannot take ownership of Information Security Management, as this would represent a conflict of interests. There needs to be segregation of roles between the groups defining and managing the process and the groups executing specific activities as part of ongoing operation. It is to the responsibility of Information Security Management to provide a 'check and balance' system to ensure effective detection and management of security issues.

The role of the Service Operation team is:

- executing security policies, standards and procedures – Service Operation teams play a role in executing these policies, standards and procedures and will work closely with the teams or departments responsible for Information Security Management. Service Operation staff are for example often the first to detect security events and are in the best position to be able to shut down and/or remove access to compromised systems
- technical assistance – some technical support may need to be provided to IT Security staff to assist in investigating security incidents and assist in production of security reports
- operational security control – for operational reasons, technical staff will often need to have privileged access to key technical areas (e.g. root system passwords, physical access to data centers or communications rooms etc). It is therefore essential that adequate controls and audit trails are kept of all such privileged activities so as to deter and detect any security events.

Experience shows that it is advisable to consider the following subjects for implementation:

- screening and vetting – consider Service Operation staff to be screened and vetted to a security level appropriate to the organization in question
- training and awareness – all Service Operation staff should be given regular and ongoing training and awareness of the organization's security policy and procedures. This should include details of disciplinary measures in place. In addition, any security requirements should be specified in the employee's contract of employment
- documented policies and procedures – Service Operation documented procedures must include all relevant information relating to security issues, extracted from the organization's overall security policy documents. Consideration should be given to the use of pragmatic, easily accessible handbooks to assist in getting the security messages out to all relevant staff. The more the handbooks are integrated in day to day processes and tools, the more effective these handbooks are.

4.6 Brief reflection on ITIL v3

At the end of this chapter let us briefly pause to consider ITIL v3. In the previous version ITIL was positioned to manage the IT infrastructure. With ITIL v3 new processes are added and new concepts are introduced. Strategy, customer assets, business goals and ROI are all concepts that are unfamiliar to the ITIL v2 community. Of course an organization could well develop in that direction but will this direction be natural and readily accepted by the business? ITIL v3 starts from a service lifecycle model. This is not about the implementation of a process but about the care that an IT service provider should take to deliver the services the business needs. This applies also to security services. But is it always clear what the business needs? Are IT and the business on an equal footing? Are they equal partners? To have a IT security strategy is one thing but is it really integrated with the business security strategy? Are the applications of new technology for business opportunities clear from the outset?

Cherry-picking
ITIL v3 combines a number of good practices, without a real integration between the many processes. Let us not forget that the methods and techniques dealt with within ITIL are not exclusively limited to IT. The complexity of ITIL may raise the bar for implementation. Use of our common sense is needed. Maintain what has worked for your organization in the past and do some cherry-picking from the new version. Keep it simple and pragmatic; above all, it should work for the business, not solely for IT. It is the results that count, not ITIL.

Information Security Management has relationships with almost all the other service management processes of this chapter and is part of many organizational activities, so it is almost impossible to operate information security as a standalone process, managed by one manager. The relationships to other processes and the management activities required to maintain an overview of information security are the most important subjects in this book. Now that ITIL version 3 has described 26 processes and four functions, their relationships with Information Security Management become quite complex and sometimes blurred. It is not always clear from the outset what the relationship is between each ITIL process and Information Security Management. In addition, new technology trends (see chapter one) have emerged but many of the challenges to manage them remain the same.

Promising developments for the future are:
• taking a more holistic and architectural approach to security
• security seen as a business enabler instead of the business prevention department
• security is an integrated part of thinking of, designing, building, transforming and operating any new or changed IT service (ITIL describes it as 'a warranty')
• more and more attention is given to a sound Risk Management approach to Information Security Management.

5 Guidelines for implementing Information Security Management

One of the greatest pitfalls in implementing Information Security Management is that it is seen as a one-time project. It is not a project, it is a process with a continual security improvement journey. Your guidelines should be the organization's policy and the organization's risk profile, not the best practice of the ISO/IEC 27002 standard.

The second pitfall is the way in which the security controls are maintained and managed. It is important to have controls and rules set up; it is even more important to manage them. New changes make it paramount that their impact should be checked against the controls already in place, not only from a technical point of view but also process, people and partners (suppliers).

In this section guidelines for implementing and improving the management process for information security are given. The CSI model is used as guidance for designing process improvement. Awareness is discussed as a crucial factor for maintaining security as well as for enabling change. Without a proper organization, with clearly defined roles and responsibilities as well as reporting lines, security will remain an issue of individual professionalism as opposite to a managed process.

Different levels of maturity in security and its management exists. This chapter shows which level fits which type of organization and how the natural growth path should be used to reach a higher level if this is required. Finally, services are often offered in diverse partnerships. It is important to assess risks that stem from the partners as well as to inspire and be inspired by partners in the area of security.

For each subject, the primary focus of Information Security Management is discussed as well as the relationships with the ITILv3 books.

5.1 Implementing or improving ITIL Information Security Management

The strategic goals for the Information Security Management process, as well as the high level process itself and the main roles and responsibilities, are defined in 'Strategy', see 4.1. The Information Security Management process is one of the Service Design processes (4.2). The Information Security Management process itself, as well as the (coordination of) controls implemented, are not implemented overnight. Implementation, as well as continuous improvement, requires careful planning.

It is important to realize that, when implementing or improving Information Security Management, it should be seen as a process – in fact, an improvement process. The improvement process can be summarized as follows:
• understanding the vision or policy by ascertaining the high-level business objectives

- assessing the current situation to identify strengths that can be built upon and weaknesses that need to be addressed
- agreeing the priorities for improvement
- detailing the process improvement program to achieve higher quality service provision
- putting measurements and metrics in place to show that the milestones have been achieved and that the business objectives and business priorities have been met
- ensuring that the momentum for quality improvement is maintained.

This is the CSI model as explained in the ITIL book on Continual Service Improvement.

Step 1: Vision
The vision must touch on all aspects of people, process, partners (suppliers) and products (tools). A good vision statement can serve three important purposes: clarify the direction of the program, motivate people to take action in the right direction and coordinate the actions of many different people. Two simple questions that can be asked when forming a vision are:
- "Can I explain this in five minutes to each of the stakeholders?"
- "Can I answer the question 'what's in it for me?' for each of the stakeholders?"

A sound vision statement is important when forming a business justification for a Information Security Management improvement program. If the program is already underway then a vision and clear set of aims can help focus more specific goals for the improvement projects and activities.

Step 2: Where are we now?
An IT organization must be able to understand where it is now. Understanding this is also important in the context of a number of perspectives:
- the business driver – do we know the business strategy and direction well enough and the risks facing the business in terms of IT?
- the technology driver – do we understand the security technology developments and how these may best be deployed to support the business? Do we understand how the business views this driver and wants to realize new business benefits offered by new secure services or security technology developments?
- the people driver – do we understand the culture and the ways we do things in our organization?

The softer aspects of people management must also be understood and the role they play in ensuring the success of any improvement program. Culture is continually named as one of the barriers in realizing any type of organizational change. What is culture? Organizational culture is often described as 'the way we do things round here'. It is the whole of the ideas, corporate values, beliefs, practices, expectations about behavior and daily customs that are shared by the employees in an organization. One could say culture is the heart of the matter or a key issue in implementing Information Security Management. Culture could support an implementation or it could be the barrier of resistance.

Step 3: Where do we want to be?
It is important that both IT and the business are in agreement about the role, and the characteristics that are required and answer for themselves the questions 'is this a "nice to have" role?' or 'is this a "need to have" role?'. 'What will be the consequences for both the business and

the IT organization if this required role is not realized?' This helps to establish a 'sense of urgency' for any Information Security Management improvement program. Defining this role also helps to give shape to the 'vision' of the future of the IT organization for the business. It is important to produce a business case and to identify a senior sponsor who supports the improvement initiative and is committed to its success. Without a sponsor there is a high risk that improvements may not be realized and funding is not made available.

Step 4: How do we get there?

If we know where we are now and where we want to be, the next question to address is: 'How do we get to where we want to be?'. If we know why we want to change and we know what we want to change, then we should also know how we want to change our quality of security.

Experience has shown that successful Information Security Management implementations depend more on the 'soft aspects' such as managing an organizational change, having awareness campaigns, managing the culture, having good project management and training people than on the 'harder' aspects like the right kind of security tools we use. Implementing Information Security Management is to embark upon an organizational change program. It is very tempting to focus only on the 'hard' aspects of security and to forget other elements such as people, process, technology and steering. It is also too easy to underestimate the scale of effort required. Support staff, users and customers will have to adopt new working practises. When any new security tool or processes is introduced, there may be initial enthusiasm for the new approach. The medium term results, however, may involve unfamiliar working practices. And lack of significant 'quick wins' may have a negative effect on the balance between costs and benefits. Drops in benefits will soon be matched with a drop in enthusiasm of the workers involved. The relevant support staff may lose interest and deny the reason for the change.

With these moods prevailing, one can see symptoms such as criticism of the people who initiated the Information Security Management implementation project, project members failing to attend meetings, not delivering results at specified deadlines and so on. The implementation of Security Management practices introduces new roles into the organization that cross traditional organizational boundaries.

Step 5: Did we get there?

To judge process performance, clearly defined objectives with measurable targets should be set from the start of the program. Confirmation needs to be sought that these objectives and the milestones set in the program have been reached and that the desired improvement in security quality has been achieved. At the completion of each significant stage of the program a Post Implementation Review (PIR) should be conducted to ensure the objectives have been met. The PIR will include a review on supporting documentation and the general awareness amongst staff of the refined processes. A comparison is required on what has been achieved against the original goals set in the project. Once this has been confirmed new improvement targets should be defined. To confirm that the milestones have been reached KPIs will need to be constantly monitored.

Step 6: How do we maintain the momentum?
The last step in this CSI-model is that the process should ensure that the momentum for security improvement is maintained by assuring that changes become embedded in the organization. This is one of the hardest part of improving (security) services.

Continual service improvement (CSI) requires resources to be allocated to CSI activities. The resources need to understand their roles and responsibilities and have the correct skill sets to execute the CSI activities. As with implementing any type of change within an organization one of the major challenges will be managing and maintaining the behavioral changes that are required. Often it requires a change in management and staff attitudes and values that continual improvement is something that needs to be done proactively and not reactively.

5.2   Awareness

The previous version of this book [CAZ] stated that "Information security is considered the biggest challenge management will face during the next decade". Now in this 21st century it is a bigger challenge than ever. Awareness campaigns are all the activities focused on a understanding of what the interests of Information Security Management mean and to guide employee, customer and public behavior towards those interests. The (coordination of) organization of awareness campaigns is a responsibility of Information Security Management.

In every Service Management implementation project, the proposed results mean that practices and procedures will have to change – even more so when dealing with Information Security Management. Information Security Management gets to the heart of the "way we do things round here". People sometimes have to change their behavior; these changes are seldom readily accepted and resistance to them is the rule rather than the exception. Users do not like having their privileges removed, even when they are not really required.

This means that it is necessary to motivate users and management to exercise discipline in adhering to security measures. Appeal for professionalism is the key. Remember that IT systems are often insecure, not for lack of good techniques but for lack of correct application of these techniques; it all comes down to the attitudes and behavior of people. Consequently, whenever possible, integrate security procedures into the normal everyday routine, and staff should come to recognize security as an enabler rather than a barrier.

Some useful pointers to running a successful awareness campaign are sketched here. Full-scale PR campaigns can be used to improve awareness; it may be beneficial to implement an awareness program designed by a professional PR agency. The most effective way is based on an annual communication plan, in which one security aspect is chosen for a period of approximately two to three months in order to inform all stakeholders about the background and progress.

People tend to see awareness as something that has to be done at the start of a Service Management implementation project. However, it is essential to communicate the progress on a regular basis throughout, using diverse media. An awareness campaign must cover the entirety of the program.

The message needs to be supported or delivered by the appropriate levels of management. Involvement of Chief Executive Officer (CEO) together with the Chief Information Officer (CIO) and Chief Information Security Officer (CISO) may be appropriate. Identifying the appropriate channels and levels requires a cultural assessment of the organization. Communication between peers in the hierarchy cannot be presumed but needs to be organized. And at distinctive occasions, visible support from senior management is needed for success.

Make sure that employees appreciate the benefits of a mature IT management to their organization, themselves and their working environment. Any security measure or change taken should fit well within the working environment and be within the organizations' capabilities. Furthermore, not only the IT people but above all the users should be able to participate in the campaign, where possible, e.g. to contribute to self-assessments, to improve on security measures and to report any adverse implications on the business.

Besides the use of reports, using the corporate magazine to inform employees about mishaps, and the response to them, has proven to be effective. Ensure the procedures are integrated in normal everyday working practice. Ensure also that those who have to work with the procedures have a hand in their development. Discipline and an awareness of why the procedures exist are equally essential. Without the latter, the former is impossible to achieve.

Few organizations have the means of enforcing discipline. A sanctions policy can help, but sanctions are not always effective, are difficult and costly to police, and can be counter-productive in the longer term. Highlighting weaknesses or imposing sanctions on staff may temporarily alert those who are involved, but the resulting awareness is usually short-lived and will create resentment. Awareness is more readily influenced by clearly visible supervision (e.g. the CISO who has a column in the newsletter of the organization to address the status of the awareness project, user reports that show an increase in satisfaction with the IT department) and by applying positive stimuli (e.g. including attendance at IT awareness campaigns and/or Information Security Management courses in job profiles).

Awareness is about communication. An awareness campaign should address everybody in the organization. However, not everybody has the same stakes, needs and interests. Start with a high level goal and then disseminate further objectives when dealing with the different needs of the different stakeholders.

Awareness is key and so is communication. Explain to employees why security is needed and why certain security measures are taken. This will prevent the situation occurring where security tends to erect barriers.

It is good practice to identify distinct audiences within the total population being addressed (e.g. (1) general employees; (2) managers; and (3) IT professionals) and to target suitable awareness materials and activities at them.

It is also good practice to plan a succession of security awareness topics, creating a rolling or continuous awareness program.

Suitable technologies and techniques should be used to get the messages across to the audiences, particularly the corporate intranet and Learning Management Systems, plus face-to-face methods such as seminars, case studies and workshops (leading into classroom teaching where appropriate).

Raising awareness is one thing; maintaining awareness is the key. In research it was found that 80 percent of all awareness campaigns failed because the campaign was too short and not continued. If you embark on awareness, it means a lifetime continual project. Information security works because of discipline, and only when supported by clear documentation and procedures. In order to achieve effectiveness, motivation is absolutely necessary. The degree of effort required for informing and educating employees depends on the national and organizational culture. However, making security work always involves an investment.

5.3   Organization of Information Security Management

Publications such as the ISO/IEC 27000 series and COBIT documents present what has to be done to organize security on a corporate level. The term 'corporate' is used here to indicate the organizational level, not the type of organization. In this section, the possible organizational structures for Information Security Management, as well as roles and responsibilities, are discussed. Answers are given to questions such as who has to manage it, what part belongs to the business, what part is for the IT department and what to do with the remainder.

This section starts with organizational structures, aligned along the triangle used below (figure 5.1). Every organization can use this to determine how to establish the Information Security Management organization. In the next section, the organizational details are positioned against the different maturity levels, to help organizations to identify what has to be in place.
Finally, the relationship between organization and governance is described.

5.3.1   Structure in the organization
In the following descriptions, the position of the functions is based on large and complex information processing organizations such as banks, insurance companies or multinational enterprises.

The most important aspect to organising information security is to clarify roles, responsibilities and accountabilities for the people concerned. This implies that those terms are clearly understood, which normally requires that the meanings and implications are spelled out in HR manuals, employment contracts, employee handbooks, job descriptions, disciplinary procedures etc.

Another key factor is to design the governance of information security, including its working and reporting relationships to other related functions and senior management. This is especially important if the information security function is truly managing the security of information assets, not only IT, since its responsibility extends across the entire organization.

The leadership of information security is yet another key differentiator between class-leading information security functions and the laggards. The leader needs strategic vision, empathy, the ability to communicate effectively with other senior managers, personal integrity and, of course, professional competence in the management discipline.

In theory there are only a few information security functions to be distinguished. In reality there is an infinite number of different implementations of functions in information security, varying from corporate wide, strategic policy writers to information security administrators for the user administration.

In defining the organization structure two approaches are used. The first approach is the abstraction level: strategy, tactical or operational. The second approach considers the disciplines involved [PVI]. In the example below, the disciplines are just IT and the rest – called 'business' to make the use of the term clearer.

The levels of abstraction give an indication of the type of control and the use of centralized steering of the organization. The disciplines fit areas of operation and allows distinguishing differences in knowledge and the type of controls or countermeasures to discuss. Just two disciplines, or areas of operation, are sketched below to keep it simple.

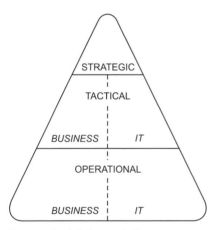

Figure 5.1: Levels in the organization

To position the security functions in organizations, the standard division of abstraction levels is used (see figure 5.1). To make the difference visible between business and IT, the dotted line is used to separate the two.

In figure 5.2, the information security functions are placed in relation to the corporate levels. At the strategic level, the corporate strategic goals or business objectives have to be interpreted and translated into information security objectives. As part of that process, decisions have to be made about all the matters that are important to implementing information security in the organization. To that end a corporate Information Security Policy gives guidance for management. The Corporate Information Security Officer (CISO) is the major player in this activity.

Information Security Architects (ISAs) design the integration of security controls in business and supporting processes, the information security architecture as well as standards, common processes and methods to be used throughout the organization. In larger organizations, two types of ISAs are found: one on the business side of the organization, the other at the IT side.

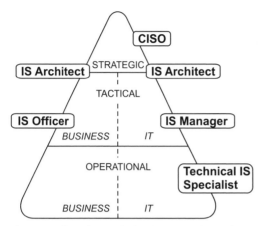

Figure 5.2: Information security functions in organizational structure

At the tactical level, the functions of Information Security Officer and Information Security Manager are equivalent. Both operate from the framework that is determined at corporate level and focus on compliance of IS standards and other references of the organization.

The Information Security Officer uses his/her knowledge of the business processes for the interpretation of the general information security standards and regulations to the specific situation.

The Information Security Manager concentrates on information and IT and uses IT management and exploitation references. Subjects such as outsourcing and certification are typical within the domain of the Information Security Manager.

The following function titles are used (table 5.1), see [PVI].

Abbreviation	Information Security Function
CISO	Corporate (or Chief) Information Security Officer
ISA	Information Security Architect – both at the Business and the IT side of the organization
ISO	Information Security Officer
ISM	Information Security Manager
TISS	Technical Information Security Specialist

Table 5.1: Information security functional roles

In organizations that are spread out over more than one location, some of the functions may have to be duplicated by location. Which functions and how many have to be available at each location depends on the nature of the business and the characteristics of the locations.

Specific ISO-roles may be defined by discipline or business support function. Typical business support functions include HR management, Legal, Facilities, Premises, Finance, Control.

At the operational level, the operational managers serve as contact points or they may appoint security focal points on their behalf.

5.3.2 Example function profiles

In the following paragraphs, profiles are given for the functions described earlier. These profiles are just examples to aid in defining function descriptions for a typical organization.

CISO

Table 5.2 shows the function profile for the Corporate Information Security Officer.

CISO	Corporate (or Chief) Information Security Officer
Department	Concern Staff
Reports to	Member of Concern Management
Goal of the function	Development of strategy and corporate policy about Information Security. Promotion and co-ordination of development of guidelines and overview of realization of corporate policy.
Functional areas	• Prepares Corporate Information Security Policy • Co-operates with ISA • Directs ISO and ISM • Co-ordinates corporate information security standards, references and guidelines • Organizes awareness programs • Co-ordinates risk assessments • Co-ordinates audits and evaluations
Competences	Master level

Table 5.2: Function profile for CISO

ISA

Table 5.3 shows the function profile for an Information Security Architect.

ISA	Information Security Architect
Department	Business Unit or IT department
Reports to	Management Team of Business Unit Director
Goal of the function	Development of information security (sub)architecture Co-ordination of security of processes and information security policy Advises management about information security
Functional areas	• Develops Business Unit architecture for Information Security • Co-operates with CISO and ISO • Supports development of corporate information security standards, references and guidelines
Competences	Master level

Table 5.3: Function profile for ISA

ISO and ISM

Table 5.4 shows the function profiles for an Information Security Officer and Information Security Manager.

ISO, ISM	Information Security Officer, Information Security Manager
Department	Officer in Business Unit; Manager in IT Department
Reports to	Management Team or Business Unit Director
Goal of the function	Supports unit or department management on tactical level Co-ordination of usage of standards and guidelines within unit or department Implementation of the Information Security Policy
Functional areas	• Initiates information security awareness programs • Develops execution guidelines • Co-operates with CISO and ISA • Supports development of corporate IS standards, references and guidelines
Competences	Master level

Table 5.4: Function profiles for ISO and ISM

TISS

Table 5.5 shows the function profile for a Technical Information Security Specialist.

TISS	Technical Information Security Specialist
Department	IT
Reports to	manager of IT Department
Goal of the function	Provide technical information security expertise for design and development of IT
Functional areas	• Designs information security in IT • Advises on information security in projects and operation
Competences	Bachelor level

Table 5.5: Function profile for TISS

5.3.3 Information security functions in relation to the maturity model

Whether information security functions are used in organizations depends on the level of maturity in information security (see section 5.5). At the lowest level of maturity, when information security is only thought of in reaction to an incident, there may be a technical expert, but it is most likely that it is coincidental or a matter of personal interest who responds to an incident. There is no structural way to extend and maintain expertise and there is no formally assigned function. In the other levels of maturity, increasing numbers of formally assigned and active functions are filled.

In table 5.6, the presence of the information security functions is shown in relation to the maturity model presented in section 5.5.

	Ad Hoc	Controlled	Service Oriented	Customer Oriented	Business Oriented
CISO			Likely	Active	Active
ISA			IT side only	Likely	Active
ISO				Likely	Active
ISM		Likely	Active	Active	Active
TISS	Not formally assigned	Formally assigned	Formally assigned	Formally assigned	Formally assigned

Table 5.6: Information security roles in relation to maturity

5.3.4 Governance

The need for governance has always existed. Nevertheless, since high profile businesses collapsed including worldwide banks during the credit crisis as well as companies such as GM, WorldCom and Enron, attention is more than ever focused on governance and risk management. Information Security Management is part of the overall governance structure, and helps to demonstrate compliance and to provide sufficient assurance.

Legislation, regulations and guidelines such as Sarbanes Oxley, Basel II and country-specific codes such as the Dutch Tabaksblatt code or the various national banks, have made directors liable. Failure in establishing, operating and maintaining risk management mechanisms will have direct personal consequences.

The shift from simple trust to formal evidence is signalling an increase of requirement for control and assurance. Information Security Management provides the control of reliability of information processing.
Since management and processes thrive on information, Information Security is a prerequisite for governance. It supports confidentiality, integrity and availability of information and information processing in a way that no other discipline can.

Governance is the set of processes that provides organizational control for internal and external usage. As part of governance, compliance with internal and/or external standards and policies is assessed. Information security is an inherent part. The assessment can be both on the processes, so the assessment of the Information Security Management process, as well on the control objectives and controls, e.g. those selected as relevant from standards such as COBIT and ISO/IEC 27001. A good practice is to embed the control framework for information security in the governance process; this is established and maintained within Information Security Management. In this way, information security management demonstrates in an integrated way, without unnecessary overhead, compliance with the security requirements and governance over information security and its management.

ISO/IEC 27001 can be used as the starting point for the ISM process as the baseline set of controls. ISO/IEC 27001 has a slightly wider scope than only information and IT. It also mandates organizational, personnel and physical security controls, although the latter are somewhat underdeveloped. The focus on business will aid in acceptance by the business part of the organization. The standard allows for both self assessment and independent certification.

There are other supporting frameworks to enable governance. (See Annex A) A combination of, for instance, ITIL and ISO/IEC 27001 or ITIL and COBIT will provide a complete and substantial IT governance, compliant with legislation and regulations.

5.4 Documentation

Information Security Management requires a documentation framework to aid in standardization and prevent inconsistencies. The documentation framework should fit the (maturity of the) organization. It must provide sufficient leeway to avoid curtailing management – having excessive rules and regulations denies management the freedom to manage. The documentation framework is maintained by Information Security Management. The framework must fit the goals set by Security Strategy (see 4.1).

Ensuring that the network is secure, for instance, is only part of the task. The organization also needs to document what has been done, for specific purposes including:
- evidencing proper design and authorisation of processes, policies etc. (the analysis that goes into preparing the documentation is often more valuable than the output)
- training and awareness of users
- compliance assessment
- reviews by third parties.

Documentation often exists online, and can include diagrams and graphics, scripts, workflows, videos, presentations, web pages, wikis, mind-maps and so on, not just paper-based documents.

Documenting security mechanisms and corresponding configurations is vital to support administration, maintenance, and any potential security compromise. It is important that security documentation is well guarded, to minimize the potential security risk, along with other forms that document how a component works—such as network diagrams and configurations.

The documentation framework consists of three layers of documentation: strategic (e.g. the information security policy document), tactical (including the common processes, tools and methods to be used throughout the organization), and operational (e.g. information security plans and handbooks for information security).

The security policy is defined for the organization as a whole; it is derived from the overall business strategy and defined as part of Security Strategy (4.1.1). The security policy document provides guidance for all employees responsible for information security. Top management should issue this document, which should contain, as a minimum:
- the objectives and scope of information security for this organization
- the goals and management principles, including how information security is being managed and a high level process description
- a definition of roles and responsibilities for information security
- the relationship with specific (security) policies and guidelines.

At the tactical level, the documentation on the methods, tools, templates and processes for common use in the organization is maintained. This is a task of Information Security Management. Examples of documentation on this level are: the security baseline, the method for risk analyses, description of the security architecture, templates for defining security settings, etc. Common processes may include security incident management; identity, authorization and access management; escalation and continuity management.

The security plan describes how the policy is being implemented for a specific system and/ or organizational unit. It describes the desired situation, with the set of security measures that should be taken. Sometimes this security plan has the characteristics of a security improvement plan: how to get from the current to the desired situation. In a security improvement plan there should be a schedule of plans for activities, controls or guidelines that should be done better or adopted in the near future.

Although security policies and guidelines comprise the majority of security documentation, procedures are equally important. These include not only the initial configuration steps, but also maintenance procedures and more importantly, the procedures to be followed in the event of a security breach.

Finally, the handbooks describe the measures for guiding the employees, either by system or by functional role. The handbook describes the specific working instructions in detail. A handbook is an operational document for day-to-day usage.

A framework can be developed using the above concept to provide a structure for the documents that describe information security. Using a structure provides overall consistency.

Table 5.7 shows the place of various documents within this documentation framework.

	Corporate	Department	Team
Why (Strategy)	Policy		
What (Tactical)	Common processes, tools, etc.	Standards, plan	
How (Operational)		Handbook, procedures	Work instructions

Table 5.7: Example documentation framework

In addition, to support the management cycle for information security, the following document structure also exists:
- the policy document, see above
- documentation that describes the current situation, derived from self- assessment, internal and external audits. The current situation is described:
  - for the organization as a whole (where it describes the progress of implementation of the security policy)
  - by unit within the organization or system (where it describes the implementation of the security plan)

- the periodic (e.g. annual) information security improvement plans. These plans describe improvement activities and corrective actions either for the organization as a whole (to improve implementation of the policy) or for specific organizational units or information systems (to improve implementation of the security plan).

Note that in the literature, the improvement plans are sometimes referred to as security plans. In this book, the security plans describe the desired situation (the set of measures that should be implemented), where security improvement plans describe how to get from the current to the desired situation.

5.5   Natural growth path through maturity levels

The first step is to be aware that something should be done: recognize the problem. Then, a plan for the first few steps is to be drafted and leadership must be strong enough to take care of implementation. In practice, it is not easy, since many priorities are imposed on the organization. It is easier to make small improvements and continue at a pace of progress that the organization can cope with. If too much pressure is put on the organization, and it is not ready for change, the improvements will not last. For information security and risk management, a natural growth path exists which follows maturity levels. These levels are defined such that it is not likely to slide back again. Stability exists in these different maturity levels.

The main steps in this process model 'path to growth' to be taken are:
- define which maturity level suits your organization best ('to be')
- assess the current level of maturity ('as is')
- follow the natural growth path from 'as is' towards 'to be'.

In this section, these maturity levels are described in more detail. Next the process model is described, and finally the natural growth path is outlined. The strategic approach towards these maturity levels is set by Security Strategy (4.1). Implementation of this strategy is a responsibility of Information Security Management. Many of the activities in implementing growth take place in Security Design (4.2), using the other processes as a vehicle towards the desired maturity.

5.5.1   Maturity levels in information security and risk management
The strategic dimension of risk management requires a method to enable adaptable information security and risk management. Using this approach, it is possible to take the strategy and ambition as the starting point and, using a process oriented approach, evolve in a controlled way to the stated ambitions while offering transparency in the achievements on the way. The maturity model in combination with the process model can meet these requirements adequately.

Risk management processes can be at several levels of maturity, while aiming at the required adaptation to meet the objectives. To facilitate this transformation, it would be desirable to balance and align the demand and supply side. The process model provides the means to reach the required balance, and provides that basis for a phased growth in a controlled, transparent manner.

Maturity model

The maturity model is based on the principle of 'thinking in maturity levels' with the related focus areas and performance indicators. Depending on the organizational context and its vision and ambition, the model can also help to provide a better view on the most appropriate process design for information security and risk management. Organizations can use the maturity model to assess the current quality and achievements of the set of security processes, controls, etc., and assess whether this set is suitable for this kind of organization. In addition, the model also shows, if needed, the next step towards the required ambition. 'Suitability for purpose' is the guiding principle. This implies that the highest level is not the target, but the level that fits the organization's requirements best. In figure 5.3 characteristics and attention points are shown, together with a sketch of the connected performance indicators. These are applied to information security, which is explained further.

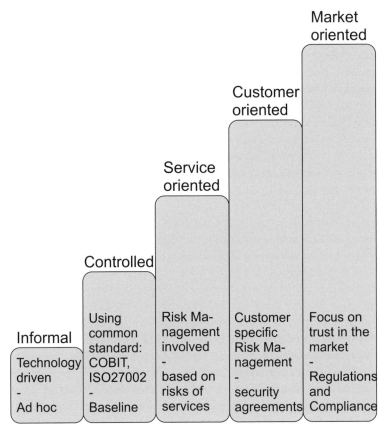

Figure 5.3: Maturity levels applied to Information Security

Ad hoc – technology driven

In this phase, information security is incident driven. If something goes wrong, a repair activity takes place. Whether or not a structural improvement is implemented depends on the professionalism of the individual who happened to be involved in fixing the incident. Activities are merely ad hoc and what happens is coincidental.

This phase is suitable for organizations with a technological approach towards information and IT, and informal management. Some security measures are implemented; the most important ones are: making backups and follow up on reported security incidents. Performance indicators focus on technical aspects.

Controlled

In this phase, a baseline set of controls for security exists. This baseline may be taken from an external source, such as the Code of Practice for Information Security Management or COBIT, a market-specific baseline, or based on experience. The organizational strategy is that the importance of information and IT is such that a known basic level of security is needed, which more or less reflects the accepted practice in their market. Security concentrates on 'Plan – Do'; it is not a complete process but focuses on the set of individual controls. A real basis for the selection of controls does not exist, other than that the set of controls is an accepted 'good practice'. The ongoing implementation of the set of controls is controlled: the organization validates, by self-assessments and internal or external audits, the status of implementation. Gaps are either addressed in improvement plans, or the consequences are accepted. The organization's performance in the quality of the implemented controls is predictable and repeatable. It can demonstrate compliance with its set of controls by management confirmation, by showing the audit results, or by certification based on a standard such as the Code of Practice.

This phase is suitable for (parts of) organizations where information and IT are to be 'in control' and where information and IT have a general, supporting role for the primary business processes. It is not the core business of the organization, but appropriate care, based on recognized standards with clear performance indicators is desired. Use of information and IT is reasonably uniform: no outstanding issues would emerge.

Note that this phase is also suitable for organizations, for example in a partnership or a value chain, that share information or IT. For large organizations it is also a common good practice to define a security baseline for all information and IT-infrastructure that is shared by the business units.

Service oriented

In the service oriented phase, risk management becomes important. The service provider is aware of the risks for its own organization that go with the service provision as well as generic risks that are inherently connected to a service. Risks are not specific for the customer or user of a service but are generic and/or concentrated on the interests of the provider. An example is provision of an email service. There are generic risks that the provider has to address since it would go out of business otherwise, which are related to availability and continuity of the service. 'Anti-virus' is sometimes added, not as a recognized risk, but as an added value service for the customer.

This phase fits organizations that offer generic services (housing, hosting, internet, standard applications) with standard performance indicators that are part of the general SLA. Services are usually offered for a wide ranges of customers. General IT service providers, telecom operators and providers of generic infrastructure fit in this phase.

Customer oriented

In this phase, risk management is specific for the customer and users of the services, who are seen as important customers; a point of contact (a customer-facing security officer) or a dedicated communication channel is put in place. Risk management is implemented to address the risks to the customer's business processes. Control objectives and controls are defined to address these specific risks; the effectiveness of the control set is made transparent to the customer. The customer and provider work together to assess and manage risks. The relationship tends towards a mutually respected partnership. Risks, control objectives and shared security processes are laid down in a security agreement. The customer requires, via its point-of-contact, to be informed about compliance with the security agreements and the agreed KPIs. 'Separation of duties' as well as 'segregation of control interest' are well-known practices, where controls are designed as a natural element in processes.

Organizations with higher risks fit this phase. Examples are: parts of government; organizations with critically important economic or social functions; internal service providers and organizations with large financial interests. The partners and providers for these types of organizations also fit in this profile. Note that these service providers are prepared to tailor their services to the risks of the customer.

Following the example of the email provider, a customer-oriented service provider would not only manage the generic risks, but would also analyze, with the customer, the risks of using email for the customer's business processes.

Market or business oriented

In this phase, risk management is focused on the added value and trust in a market as a whole, trust in the industry involved, an economic value chain or a part of society. In this phase a common governance structure exists. Proactive communication takes place and performance is so predictable and transparent that continued trust is reasonably assured. The organizations in such a sector are individually or systematically so important that their (mis)behavior can have a devastating influence on the sector as a whole. The assurance framework is specific for the sector and is laid down in publicly available rules and regulations. Compliance with this control framework is organized within the sector or by means of an appointed authority or overseeing body.

The financial sector fits this phase. Oversight is done through the national Central Bank or other financial authorities. Control frameworks are set by organizations such as the ECB and Bank for International Settlement. Organizations in healthcare also fit here. Companies that are listed on a stock exchange are also obliged to meet some of the criteria here.

5.5.2 Process model 'path to growth'

One of the basic principles is 'maintaining an appropriate balance': risk management must provide the balance between the demand and the supply-chain risk (or: balancing risks in the value chain). Depending on the 'to be'-situation, the natural growth path from the current situation ('as is') to the 'to be'-situation can be followed. Each stage in such a growth path must be designed so that the organization does not slip back to its old situation.

The growth path is taken in five steps (figure 5.4):
- **Step 1:** Ambition level. Determine the desirable or required maturity level of your organization as well as that of your partners (these do not have to be the same).
- **Step 2:** Initial assessment. The purpose of this step is to assess the current 'as is'-situation, the roadmap to the destination and to document the Plan of Action. The gap between the current and required situation is defined. The Plan of Action is set up with improvement activities that are grouped by maturity level. The Plan of Action also determines how progress is monitored and when intermediate assessments take place. The grouping of required improvements activities by maturity level guarantees that the organization follows the natural growth path.
- **Step 3:** Intermediate assessments follow the progress of the improvement activities.
- **Step 4:** Final assessment. Its purpose is to assess whether the required level is reached and if residual risks are acceptable.
- **Step 5:** From project to process: along the road of improvement a security and risk management process is established. An indispensable element in each process is to build in assessments on a regular basis (self-assessments, peer and management reviews, internal control, internal/external audits).

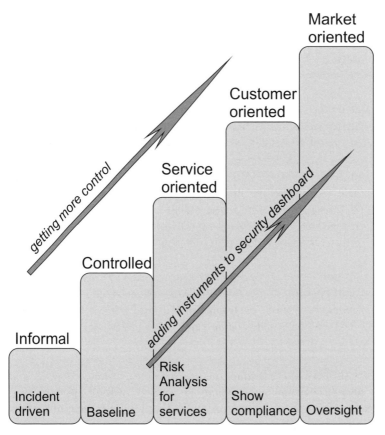

Figure 5.4: Path to growth

5.5.3   Key elements of the process model 'path to growth'

In this section some key elements by maturity level are given as illustrations. For each level the same elements are described: management and organization; IT infrastructure; people and culture; processes.

Technology oriented – 'ad hoc'

There is no information security policy. Everything that happens is based on each employee's personal professionalism and is more or less a coincidence. At least two controls exist: proper backup and follow-up on security incidents.

Management and organization does not include formal responsibilities for risk or security. Each professional, within the primary functions as well as in IT, human resources management, legal, facilities management takes up their own 'assumed' part.

The **IT infrastructure** is made up of small ad hoc infrastructures with uncontrolled parts and no defined ownership.

For the **people and culture** aspects, although no specific guidelines for risk and security exist, the culture of the organization may be helpful for the right things to happen.

There are no defined **processes**.

Controlled

A Handbook for Information Security describes the policy and the baseline set of security controls. The organization has implemented the baseline. The controls are derived from an external recognized standard and thereafter tailored to the needs of the organization. Selection of these controls was not based on an analysis of requirements but on accepted 'good practices' in the market, combined with some high level judgment about whether a specific control suits the organization. This is a simple assessment of the usefulness of a control in view of perceived risks. The organization wants to be on more or less the same level as comparable competitors and/or its customers. It has a clear view of the implementation of the baseline, since regular assessments and audits take place. Any gaps are treated according to a plan of action.

Management and organization defines accountability for Information security with the head of IT or Information Security Manager. Other responsibilities, for operational departments as well as for supporting functions, are defined. An organization is defined in which coordination of activities takes place based on both a process view (annual cycle) and a project view (Improvement Plan).

In the **IT infrastructure** all external connections are controlled, e.g. through firewalls and remote access facilities. Identification and authentication for access to networks, platforms and applications is always enforced. Logical access control and authorization management are fully dependent on line management control.

From a **people and culture** perspective, the importance of the human factor is recognized. Regular campaigns to stimulate desired behavior and security awareness take place. There are codes of conduct for personnel for the proper use of email, internet, external communication and devices or facilities from the organization for professional use.

Processes are in place: The information security management system is defined and implemented. It is the starting point of every day's work. Audits take place on a regular basis, and certification can be considered. In communication with partners, customers and suppliers, reference is made to the baseline. Since the baseline is based on a recognized standard, stakeholders have a general feeling of what can be expected. Additional assurance can be gained through, as said, certification and independent audits. Within the organization at least common processes are defined for incident management, authorization management and continuity management. The organization is aware of applicable rules and regulation, including legislation on privacy protection, computer crime and protection of intellectual property rights.

The information security policy contains, as a minimum, the information security management system (with an annual process cycle), organizational structure, roles and responsibilities in general terms, the security baseline, organized improvement activities.

Service oriented
'Risk management' is added. Preferably one method for risk management is used throughout the organization, but for good reasons several accepted methods may exist. The risk management is described and addresses at least:
- risk analysis
- risk prioritization
- risk treatment (accept, mitigate, transfer)
- acceptance of residual risks.

At this level of maturity, risk management mainly looks at the generic risks that are inherently related to the service offering. The general approach is: if a risk materializes, what would be the impact for the service provider?

Accepted standards for risk management are already in place. Although tooling can be helpful, also to make analysis all through the organization comparable, it is recommended to start with manual approaches.

For **management and organization**, responsibilities for risk management are added.

The **service infrastructure** is viewed from a service perspective: risks relating to services are known, e.g. based on the Business Impact Assessment. The results of risk analysis are documented and maintained on a regular basis. Residual risk acceptance is a formal exercise.

For the organization's **people and culture**, employees are aware of the service-specific risks for the organization.

The information security management system now also contains an additional **process** – Risk Management. Risk assessments take place at defined points in the development process (design, construction), transition (testing, formal acceptance, change management) and hand over to everyday operations. Risk analyses are maintained on a regular basis. Auditors also look at the processes as auditable objects.

Risk management is added to the information security policy.

Customer oriented

Risk management is focused on the risks for customers. More customer-dependent risk management methods may have to be supported. Service providers at this level of maturity focus on the requirements for risk management set by the customers.

The general approach is: if a risk materializes, what would be the impact for the customer?

A common risk management process between service provider and customer is established. The risk management processes of the individual organizations are connected, providing input (status of compliance, residual risks) and using the output.
Assurance is also customer specific. First, the service providers states the assurance that is offered as a standard part of the service provision, e.g. compliance with a baseline. Customers define what level of additional assurance they require.

In **management and organization**, a point of contact is established for each customer for risk management, sometimes referred to as the customer Risk and Compliance Information Security Manager.

The **information infrastructure** is focussed on the information and processing requirements that are derived from the business drivers and business processes of the customer. These requirements include those for security and continuity. The security of or offered by the information infrastructure reflects these requirements.

There are **common processes**: beside the common processes for incident, access control/ authorization and continuity another process is defined for risk management. An example to implement this is to agree on regular workshops for professionals from each organization to assess risks.

For the **people and culture** aspects, employees are aware of the risks for the customers.

Risk Management is now a **customer oriented process** and is added to the information security policy.

Business or market oriented

Risk management is focused on the risks for the market as a whole. Although more risk management methods may be supported, service providers at this level of maturity usually focus on a specific market sector, such as banking.

The general approach is: if a risk materializes, what would be the impact for the market?

Common rules and regulations that aim at stability and maintaining trust exist and apply to all participants in the market. The interests of consumers and other businesses that rely on or depend on this market are taken into account. A governance framework is established, aiming at enforcing compliance or signalling non-compliance.

Management and organization: a common governance structure is established in which one or more authorities provide oversight and are responsible for safeguarding stability. Participants in such a market require a license to operate, provided by an authority. On a regular basis, the participants provide assurance to the authority regarding compliance with the rules and regulations. Non-compliances as well as specific incidents are to be reported. Key personnel is known to the authorities and possibly screening takes place.

The responsibilities of top management include: reporting on management supervision regarding risk management and accountability.

Governance **processes** are established providing continual assurance of compliance or early detection of non-compliance.
Risk management is also concerned with the risks for the market as a whole as well as the social interest of malfunctioning. Loss of trust of consumers or politics are examples of manageable risks.

Separation of duties conforms to rules and regulations. Separation of functions is embedded in authorization and access management.

Common **processes** exist between top management and authorities to report on the effective arrangements for, for example, risk management and business continuity management (capacity management, business continuity en contingency planning). Walk-throughs and disaster recovery tests are scheduled.

A structure of internal supervision, and internal and external auditing covers all relevant objects on a regular basis.

The Information and IT infrastructure
Top management, based on the results from the governance processes, reports externally on the effective implementation of the information security and continuity policy as well as the status of implementation of security services. The security architecture provides transparency in the mapping from functional requirements, as derived from the defined risks and objectives, to technical implementation and operational management.

People and culture: employees may be screened and are required to sign confidentiality agreements as well as codes of conduct. An example is that employees are not allowed to hold stocks or have other interests in certain companies.

5.6   Pitfalls and success factors

From experiences of other organizations, it is easy to learn what to do and what to avoid. The pitfalls and success factors described in this section are universal and equally valid for different kinds of organizations. By avoiding the problem areas, implementing and maintaining Information Security Management becomes easier.

5.6.1   Pitfalls
From experiences with all kinds of organizations over the last decades, the following standard pitfalls have been noted:
- **insufficient management involvement** – deciding about what security controls will have to be implemented is like making decisions about investments. In both cases money will be spent. Since managers are holders of budgets, they have to be involved in the entire process of defining the best security counter measures. If there are too few managers involved, this will cause delay in making the right decisions. Another reason why managers are important is the position they have in their department. They are seen as examples. If managers do not follow the (security) rules, employees in their department will refuse to follow them too.
- **ambition level set too high** – often the professionals defining and implementing information security (management) want to be certain that everything is complete and as good as it can be. This will certainly result in delay in achieving results; the organization will also be overwhelmed with rules, regulations and new procedures. It is advisable to use a phased approach in which small steps are taken, which gives the organization time to get used to the new things. At the same time it allows for fine tuning the phases.
- **the 'Ivory Tower' pitfall** is related to the previous one. In this case, the professionals develop solutions in isolation from the business and its processes. The only way to design solutions is to work in close co-operation with the people who have to perform them.
- **'it is not my department'** is the most frequently heard excuse to do nothing. Information security is everyone's "department". Originally the IT department was responsible for information security. With the new regulations and managers being held liable for mismanagement, the shift to the business as the more important player is visible.
- **invisible security** – when no mishaps in the organization are seen, there is a perception that everything is going well. If there are no incidents, there is no lack of security. Staff complain that they have to follow difficult and time consuming procedures for information security that are perceived as unnecessary. The basis of security awareness is knowing why it is necessary. The next thing is knowing what has to be done.
- **inconsistencies** – when dealing with security in an organization there are links between departments, processes and systems. When managing that security, it is crucial to recognize the difference in security level in the parts of the organization. The weakest links are made by inconsistencies in rules, regulations and procedures.
- **exceptions become permanent** – this is related to the previous pitfall. By definition, exceptions should be temporary; with well known expiry dates. It requires considerable effort from Information Security Management to enforce the temporary nature of exceptions. This is valid for workarounds that are quicker or easier than the original procedures.
- **add-on security** – a vault with a padlock will not work as well as one with an integrated locking mechanism. Built in or integrated security is the ultimate goal, which means that early in the design process the security requirements have to be available and security functionality is designed in.

- **lack of evaluation and feedback** – inspections, auditing and discussing the results is the closing part of the full circle of Information Security Management.

The most common pitfall is a lack of (senior) management interest. This varies from not setting the right examples and showing the wrong attitude to refusing to attend workshops.

Part of the solution to avoid this lack of interest lies in keeping senior management well informed about the level of security, by having a comprehensive security plan in which 'risks' are balanced against the measures taken. This is a task of Information Security Management.

5.6.2 Success factors
There are also success factors:
- **involvement** of the people processing the information is very important. They know how to handle it and they know what will work. They also know what is right and what is wrong with their information processing. That knowledge is valuable and tapping that source will reduce the time spent on finding requirements in system documentation. It is a good practice to have procedures drawn up by the users, rather than defining procedures in isolation. It also makes acceptance at the working level easier to achieve.
- **awareness** is crucial. Information security comprises of more organizational than technical countermeasures. In order to have everybody follow the procedures, motivation is essential. The easiest way to fuel that motivation is by information. Knowing why information security is used is the first half of awareness. Knowing how to use it well is the second half.
- **clear responsibility** and being held accountable for safeguarding the reliability and value of information is essential. The 'one captain rules the ship' principle also works with managers with information security. The more people are responsible, the less responsibility there is. Further, it helps when accountability issues have to be raised. Sanctions must be applied, if required, in order to have information security taken seriously.

5.7 Partnerships and outsourcing

Maintaining information security within the boundaries of the organization can be a considerable task; when more than one organization is involved, the task becomes more difficult. There always will be a certain amount of mistrust because of not precisely knowing what the other party is doing.

Both with partners as with outsourcing, part of the information or information processing is kept outside direct control. This means that assurances have to be sought to ensure that everything will be as secure as is necessary.

5.7.1 Partnerships
Organizations have links with all kinds of other organizations, sometimes in other countries. Those links can be with governmental agencies, suppliers and customers; they may vary from simple store-and-forward messaging through use of distant applications to direct queries and updates of databases.
These kinds of links improve efficiency and productivity dramatically; it resolves the problem of re-entering data that is already available digitally.

However, coupling of IT requires co-ordination of information security controls to prevent weak spots or inconsistencies. Generally, interfaces are the most challenging parts for information security. It is often possible to misuse a connection, place digital wire taps or exploit procedures to gain unauthorized entrance.

This means that when information security crosses organizational boundaries Information Security Management on both sides has to work together.

ISO 27002 (paragraph 6.2) gives a list of issues to be taken into account when allowing external parties access to the organization's information or information processing.

Part of those issues cover controls to be in place, the remainder involves organization and management:
- procedures to protect organizational assets, including information, software and hardware
- procedures to determine whether any compromise of the assets, e.g. loss or modification of information, software and hardware, has occurred
- controls to ensure the return or destruction of information and assets at the end of, or at an agreed point in time during, the agreement
- a clear reporting structure and agreed reporting formats
- a clear and specified process of change management
- an authorization process for user access and privileges, including administration and reporting on changes and on irregularities
- arrangements for reporting, notification, and investigation of information security incidents and security breaches, as well as violations of the requirements stated in the agreement
- the right to audit responsibilities defined in the agreement, to have those audits carried out by a third party, and to enumerate the statutory rights of auditors
- service continuity requirements, including measures for availability and reliability, in accordance with an organization's business priorities
- involvement of the third party with subcontractors, and the control objectives or security controls these subcontractors need to implement;
- conditions for renegotiation/termination of agreements:
  - a contingency plan should be in place in case either party wishes to terminate the relation before the end of the agreements
  - renegotiation of agreements if the security requirements of the organization change
  - current documentation of asset lists, licenses, agreements or rights relating to them.

It is a good practice to use this list of subjects as checklist for preparing Service Level Agreements in expanding cross-border information security with other organizations.

5.7.2 Information security and outsourcing IT services
When outsourcing IT services, most organizations are trying to find the right company to do the job. Functionality and price are the dominant factors. However, the risks involved may become more significant because of dependence on information and information processing. The more access there is to IT assets, the greater the risk of something unwelcome happening. This is not merely a matter of competitive disadvantage: a service provider that discloses financial information or releases maliciously modified information could be held liable. An organization

that outsources information processing without maintaining control over information security may be held liable because of mismanagement. It is likely that customers will suffer from security breaches as well.

The checklist in the previous paragraph is valid in outsourcing situations as well as in partnerships in IT.

It is important to address these security issues in a (separate) part of the SLA. Mere availability of a ISO/IEC 27001 certificate from the provider is not sufficient. Next to the security requirements and assurance that these are met, audits at regular intervals are required to ensure insight in the way information security is maintained. ISO/IEC 20000 requires that an organization has management control over its suppliers.

Annex A: Information Security Management and standardization

A number of standards have been published that aid in the implementation and application of Information Security Management. The use of standards is important because it enables comparison between organizations, it provides common communication and it serves as the basis for public discussions and training.

The standards will also serve as common understanding to be used by everyone with access to them.

There are three major types of standards:
- formal standards – issued by formal standardization bodies as assembled in the International Standardization Organization (ISO)
- best practices – are issued by ISO or organizations of professionals. They are not used for certification but can be used for benchmarking. It is important to translate those standards to the typical situation of the organization instead of adopting them unamended. This is valid for the ITIL best practices, for COBIT and for ISO/IEC 27002
- ad hoc standards are often technical standards, issued by manufacturers.

A.1   ISO/IEC 27000 series

The ISO/IEC 27000 series of standards deal with information security, and are the products of JTC1/SC27 the sub-committee responsible for standards in the domain of IT security techniques. So far the Code of Practice for Information Security Management (ISO/IEC 27002, formerly ISO/IEC 17799) is their best known product.

A complete series of standards about IT security techniques is foreseen. For more information see www.iso.org.

A.1.1   ISO/IEC 27001 – Information Security Management Systems – Requirements

Published in 2005, and based on part 2 of BS7799, it describes the (closed loop) management system for information security. It enables continuous improvement, just like the quality system in ISO/IEC 9001 and the environmental control system in ISO/IEC 14001.

All these management systems are defined in a singular consistent matter. This makes it easier to implement an information security management system, for instance, once a quality system is in place. The details of the processes are similar and the use of handbooks and written procedures is already known in the organization. The implementation of the quality system also requires the same type of awareness communication that is needed for Information Security Management.

The cornerstones of ISO/IEC 27001 are the Statement of Applicability (SofA) and the regular management review. The SofA is basically the list of controls. It has to be written against ISO/IEC 27002 and includes the reasons for exclusion of the controls that are not implemented. A risk analysis report must show the results of the assessment of the risks, therefore indicating the reasons for implementing controls.

Next to a very formal certification process through official certification bodies, self-assessment is possible against the standard. It will provide comparable information like a benchmark on the status of implementation of the Information Security Management system.

This standard is to be used by those professionals who are responsible for implementing and maintaining the ISMS.

ISO/IEC 27001 is the only auditable international standard that defines the requirements for an Information Security Management System (ISMS). The standard is designed to ensure the selection of adequate and proportionate security controls.

A.1.2   ISO/IEC 27002 – Code of Practice
In spite of its full name (Code of Practice for Information Security Management), it is a best practice for information security controls and a little bit of management. For more information on the management system, the 27001 standard provides better reading, and gives concise requirements Information Security Management systems should comply with.

This Code of Practice covers 133 security controls subdivided in 11 sections, varying from the corporate information security policy via security incident handling to acquisition, development and maintenance of information systems.

Those controls are put together by the committee that wrote the standard as they deemed appropriate; they are not the result of a risk analysis for a given situation in a certain organization. There is no organization anywhere that requires all 133 controls to secure its information processes; they will require a subset of those controls and will also need a few additional ones that are not covered in the standard.
It is clearly stated in the standard that a risk analysis – or risk assessment as it is called in 27002 – is always required before deciding which controls to use. In that process a further assessment will reveal the priority of implementation based upon business need or implementation costs. Process management will ultimately decide on implementation versus taking risks.

The Code of Practice is written for IT and information security professionals who are responsible for implementing security controls; it is not written for business or process managers.

The standard is written from an information security point of view, not from an IT perspective, which means that subjects such as configuration control or change management are only briefly covered. The same is true for physical security. The subject is dealt with in a separate chapter; however the coverage is insufficient to use as guide for implementing physical security.

A.1.3 ISO/IEC 27005:2008 – Information Security Risk Management

This international standard provides guidelines for Information Security Risk Management in an organization, supporting in particular the requirements of an information security management system complying with ISO/IEC 27001. It does not provide any specific method or technique; it is left to the organization to choose their approach to risk management.

The standard gives a detailed overview of the steps to be taken to manage risks. The subjects covered are risk assessment, risk treatment, risk acceptance, risk communication and risk monitoring and review.

The standard relies heavily on ISO/IEC 27001 and 27002; it is relevant to managers and staff concerned with information security risk management within an organization.

A.2 ISO/IEC 13335:2004 – Management of information and communications technology security

The standard consists of two parts:
- Part 1 – Concepts and models for information and communications technology security management
- Part 2 – Techniques for information and communications technology security management.

Parts 3, 4 and 5 have been produced as Technical Reports and have not so far been released as standards.

Part 1 provides a high-level management overview of management of information security. It is aimed at managers and those who have responsibility for IT security or for an organization's IT security program.

After chapters dealing with scope and definitions, chapters 3 and 4 provide an overview of security concepts, objectives and policy elements. In chapter 5 organizational aspects are discussed and finally in chapter 6, some IT security management functions are listed. Part 2 of ISO/IEC 13335 provides operational guidance on IT security. Together these parts can be used to help identify and manage aspects of IT security.

A.3 ISO 7498-2 – OSI Security Architecture

Standard ISO 7498-2:1989 is one of the documents in the ISO 7498 series that describe the basic reference model for Open Systems Interconnection (OSI). It was released in 1989.

It is aimed at the security controls that must be established to protect information exchange between the application processes of interconnected, heterogeneous computer systems.

Part 2 defines the general security-related architecture elements such as services and security mechanisms. It serves as a guideline to allow secure communications, within the framework of the OSI Reference model.

In chapter 8, OSI security management is described in three distinct categories:
- system security management
- security service management
- security mechanism management.

In addition, security of OSI management is covered.

Table A.1 lists the activities that fit within the three categories. It provides an overview of the subjects covered in the standard.

Category	Activity
System Security Management	
	Overall Security Policy Management
	Interaction with other OSI management functions
	Event Handling Management
	Security Audit Management
	Security Recovery Management
Security Service Management	
	Assessment of Target Security for the service
	Assessment of the security mechanisms to employ
	Negotiation of available security mechanisms
	Invocation of the specific security mechanisms
	Interaction with other security service management functions
Security Mechanism Management	
	Key Management
	Encryption Management
	Digital Signature Management
	Access Control Management
	Data Integrity Management
	Authentication Management
	Traffic Padding Management
	Routing Control Management
	Notarization Management

Table A.1: Security categories and activities

This standard is aimed at confidentiality and integrity. Availability and continuity are lacking.

It shows that since its first release, ISO 7498-2 has not been updated. Development in information technology has changed considerably since 1989. Commonplace elements like the Internet, browser technology or cloud computing have not been considered. The lists of security services and the overview of security mechanisms are outdated.

A.4 ISO/IEC 20000:2005 – Service Management

A brief introduction

Effective service management delivers high levels of customer service and customer satisfaction. To do so many organizations across the globe have adopted ITIL, as a best practice framework for IT Service Management but ITIL does not set out the minimum set of requirements for IT Service Management. ISO/IEC20000 and its predecessor BS15000 does this, so now all IT Service Management service providers know what they should aspire to.

What is ISO/IEC 20000 and what is the advantage for a user?

ISO/IEC20000 is a standard to promote the adoption of an integrated process approach to the effective delivery of IT services. It is a set of 'controls' against which an organization can be assessed for effective IT Service Management processes. The standard is a significant step towards IT service delivery becoming mature and stable across organizational and national borders. Business and customers can have more confidence if their IT service provider is ISO/IEC20000 certified.

What is the purpose of ISO/IEC20000?

Part 1 of ISO/IEC 20000 defines the requirements for a service provider to deliver managed services of an acceptable quality for its customers. Part 2 of ISO/IEC20000 provides guidance to auditors and offers assistance to service providers planning service improvements.

'Part 1' is a set of mandatory requirements. The requirements are stated as 'SHALLS' against which an organization can be assessed for effective IT Service Management processes. 'Part 2' gives guidance and recommendations for effective IT Service Management processes. This guidance is in the form of 'SHOULDS'. ISO/IEC20000 certification means an organization can now prove that they are deploying best practice, because an independent external evaluation against the ISO/IEC20000 standard has been carried out by an approved registered certification body (RCB).

What are the main parts of ISO/IEC20000?

Part 1 of the standard defines the requirements for an organization to deliver managed services of an acceptable quality for its customers. The standard specifies not only a number of closely related service management processes (section 5 through section 10), but also requirements for the management system (section 3), planning and implementing service management (section 4) and planning and implementing new or changed services (section 5). Section 1 and 2 are introduction and terms and definitions.

It is worthwhile to consider that requirements for a management system (section 3) provide the framework for all other sections. For instance management control of a process consists of:
• knowledge and control of the inputs
• knowledge, use and interpretation of the outputs
• definition and measurement of metrics (performance indicators)
• demonstration of objective evidence of accountability for process functionality
• definition, measurement and review of process improvements.

The relationships between the processes (section 5 through 10) depend on the application within an organization. The list of objectives and controls contained in this specification is not exhaustive, and an organization may consider that additional objectives and controls are necessary to meet their particular business needs. The nature of the business relationship between the service provider and business will determine how the requirements in this standard are implemented to meet the overall objective. Another warning: compliance with this standard does not itself confer immunity from legal obligations.

Readers who are familiar with ITIL processes will easily recognize the processes defined in the ISO/IEC 20000 standard.

ISO/IEC 20000 relevance to Information Security Management?
One of the processes an organization has to be in control of is the "Information Security Management". The objective of this process is "To manage information security effectively within all service activities". Organizations already certified to ISO/IEC 27001 will satisfy the requirements of ISO20000 Information Security Management. Within Part 1 there are 9 norms for this process:
1. management with appropriate authority approve an information security policy
2. management communicate an information security policy to all relevant personnel and customers where appropriate
3. appropriate security controls operate to implement the requirements of the information security policy
4. appropriate security controls also operate to manage risks associated with access to the service or systems
5. security controls are documented. The documentation describes the risks to which the controls relate, and the manner of operation and maintenance of the controls. The impact of changes on controls is assessed before changes are implemented
6. arrangements that involve third-party access to information systems and services are based on a formal agreement that defines all necessary security requirements
7. security incidents are reported and recorded in line with incident management procedure as soon as possible
8. procedures are in place to ensure that all security incidents are investigated, and management action taken
9. mechanisms are in place to enable the types, volumes and impacts of security incidents and malfunctions to be quantified and monitored, and to provide input to the service improvement plan.

A.5   ISF: The standard of Good Practice for Information Security

The Standard represents part of the International Security Forum (ISF) information risk management suite of products and is based on material, research, and the knowledge and practical experience of ISF members worldwide. The ISF is an association of organizations in the commercial and public sectors, for the purposes of addressing security and related issues concerned with the use of information and information technology. All results such as reports, briefings, meetings and conferences are for the benefit of the members, with the exception of the Standard of Good Practice, which is released through www.securityforum.org.

This standard is said to be in line with publications such as COBIT 4.1 and ISO/IEC 27002.

The standard contains a section on security management from an information security point of view. It shows high level principles and objectives that enable implementation and operation of security management to meet the basic information security principles. Care should be taken to conduct a risk analysis to support decisions about controls and measures. ISF publishes risk analysis methodologies, which are available only to members of ISF.

A.6   SABSA

SABSA® (Sherwood Applied Business Security Architecture) is a model for developing risk-driven enterprise information security architectures and intends to deliver security infrastructure solutions that support critical business initiatives. SABSA has evolved since 1995 to meet a variety of business needs including risk management, information assurance, governance, and continuity management. SABSA aims to ensure that the specific needs of an enterprise are met and that security services are designed, delivered and supported as an integral part of the business and IT management infrastructure.

At the heart of it is this SABSA Matrix Model (figure A.2)

This model is also used in environments that have used the Zachman IT Architecture Framework and Open Group's TOGAF, COA and Jericho models amongst others.

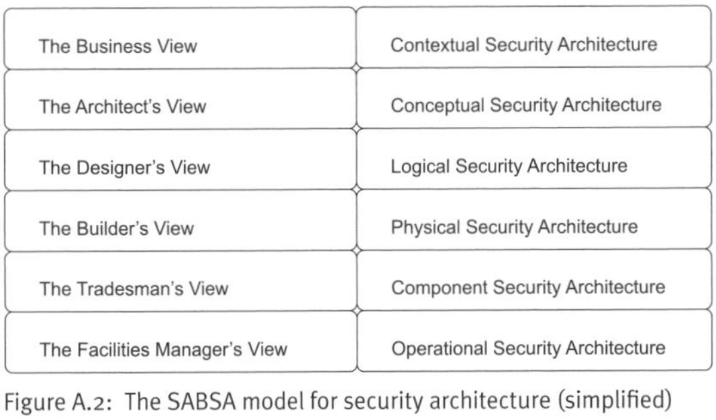

The Business View	Contextual Security Architecture
The Architect's View	Conceptual Security Architecture
The Designer's View	Logical Security Architecture
The Builder's View	Physical Security Architecture
The Tradesman's View	Component Security Architecture
The Facilities Manager's View	Operational Security Architecture

Figure A.2: The SABSA model for security architecture (simplified)

A characteristic of the SABSA model is that the starting point of security design is an analysis of the business requirements, especially those in which security has an enabling function. SABSA

	Assets (What)	Motivation (Why)	Process (How)	People (Who)	Location (Where)	Time (When)
Contextual	The Business	Business Risk Model	Business Process Model	Business Organization and Relationships	Business Geography	Business Time Dependencies
Conceptual	Business Attributes Profile	Control Objectives	Security Strategies and Architectural Layering	Security Entity Model and Framework	Security Domain Model	Security-Related Lifetimes and Deadlines
Logical	Business Information Model	Security Policies	Security Services	Entity Schema and Privilege Profiles	Security Domain Definitions and Associations	Security Processing Cycle
Physical	Business Data Model	Security Rules, Practices and Procedures	Security Mechanisms	Users, Applications and the User Interface	Platform and Network Infrastructure	Control Structure Execution
Component	Detailed Data Structures	Security Standards	Security Products and Tools	Identities, Functions and ACL's	Processes, Nodes, Addresses and Protocols	Security Step Timing and Sequencing
Operational	Assurance of Operational Continuity	Operational Risk Management	Security Service Management and Support	Application and User Management and Support	Security of Sites, Networks and Platforms	Security Operations Schedule

Table A.3: SABSA master matrix

intends to create a chain of traceability through the strategy and concept, design, implementation, and ongoing 'manage and measure' phases of the lifecycle to ensure that the business mandate is preserved. The model is layered, with the top layer being the business requirements definition stage. At each lower layer a new level of abstraction and detail is developed, going through the definition of what is referred to as the conceptual architecture, logical services architecture, physical infrastructure architecture and finally at the lowest layer, the selection of technologies and products (component architecture).

A.7   COBIT

The Control Objectives for Information and related Technology is a set of best practices for IT created by ITGI (IT Governance Institute) and ISACA (Information Systems Audit and Control Association). It provides a framework for users, managers and auditors with best practices, processes and generally accepted measures aimed at optimized use of IT and developing appropriate IT governance and control.

The document is internationally accepted and used as reference for consultants, managers and auditors alike.

COBIT 4.1 mentions 34 high level processes that cover 210 control objectives. The objectives are structured in four domains that resemble some of the lifecycle phases of ITIL.

Although Information Security Management is not covered as a whole, the importance of it is emphasized in the 'ensure systems security' process (numbered DS5). Control objectives of the system security process are similar to the activities of Information Security Management discussed earlier. Focus is on IT management.

One of the benefits of COBIT is the application of a Maturity Model. For each process it is defined what the characteristics are of each of the five maturity levels. Ranging from zero: non-existent to five – optimized, it is clearly defined how organizations should behave. When information security maturity is made part of it, Information Security Management will benefit from the structural approach towards a more mature IT management.

COBIT does reference a Risk Analysis as basis for information security measures or controls, however there is no mention about any kind of a statement of applicability or risk analysis result that is updated regularly.

COBIT provides a control framework at the highest level of IT governance based on a generic IT process model. For more detailed, practitioner level processes, ITIL and ISO/IEC 27000 series standards are useful.

The table below sketches were ITIL v3 Information Security Management activities can best be placed in COBIT processes. So, it is not a mapping but presents an indication of where ITIL ISM subjects fit best.

ITIL v3 Information Security Management	COBIT
Service Strategy • Security Strategy • Maturity Level for security • Assurance issues – risk, auditing and compliance • Demand supply relationship in risk management • Principles for security service design and security architectures • Security service portfolio • Demand management support for information security management • Financial management / service economics support for ISM	PO: 'Plan and Organise' • PO1 Define strategic plan • DS1 Define and manage service levels • PO4, ME2, ME4 address assurance; AI2.3 addresses auditability • PO9 Assess and manage risks • PO1.6 IT portfolio management • PO5 Manage IT investment
Service design • Security Service Level Management; • Security Service Catalogue Management; • Supplier Management and ISM support • Capacity Management and ISM support • Availability Management • IT Service Continuity Management	PO4.1: IT process framework • DS1 Service level management • DS1.2 Definition of services • DS2: Manage third party services • DS13.3: IT infrastructure monitoring • DS3.4: resource availability management • DS4: Ensure continuous availability
Service transition • Change Management and ISM • ISM and Service Asset & Configuration Management • Release & Deployment Management and ISM • Service Transition Planning & Support and ISM • Service Validation & Testing • Evaluation and ISM • Knowledge Management and ISM	Most in AI • AI6 manage changes • DS9 Manage the configuration • AI7 Install and accredit solutions and changes • AI3-7 • AI3 to AI 7 • AI7 Install and accredit solutions and changes • AI6.2 Impact assessment, prioritisation andauthorisation • AI4.2-4.3 Knowledge transfer
Continual Service Improvement • The 7-step improvement process for ISM • Service reporting support for ISM • Service measurement support for ISM: security measuring/metrics • Security Service Level Management • CSI Methodes and tools to support ISM	PO 8.5 Continious Improvement • PC6 Process performance improvement • DS1.5 Monitoring and reporting of service level achievement • DS1.5 Monitoring and reporting of service level achievement • DS1 Define and manage service levels • ME1.1 Monitoring approach
Service operation • Event management and ISM • Request fulfilment and ISM • Security Incident management and process • Problem management and ISM • Access management and ISM • Application management and ISM • Technical management and ISM • IT Operations and ISM	DS13 Manage operations • DS3, DS8, DS13 (manage...) • AI6 Manage changes • DS8 Manage service desk and incidents • DS10 Manage problems • DS5.3 Identity management • Part of DS13 • Part of DS13 • Part of DS13

Assurance topics in COBIT are covered in the following sections:

COBIT assurance topics	ITIL v3 Information Security Management
PO 4.8 Responsibility for Risk, Security and Compliance PO 4.11 Segregation of duties PO 2.3 Data classification scheme PO 2.4 Integrity management PO 6.2 Enterprise risk and control framework PO 9 Assess and manage IT risks PO 9.1 IT Risk management framework PO 9.2 Establish risk context	Service Strategy support for Information Security Management
AI 1.2 Risk analysis reporting AI 2.3 Application control and auditability AI 2.4 Application security and availability AI 3.2 Infrastructure resource protection and availability AI 6.2 Impact assessment, prioritisation and authorisation	All sections
DS2.3 Supplier risk management DS3 Manage performance and capacity DS4 Ensure continuous service DS5 Ensure systems security DS 5.1 Management of IT security DS 5.5 Security testing, surveillance and monitoring DS7.1 Education, training, awareness.. DS12 Manage the physical environment DS 13.4 Sensitive documents and output devices	Primarily Service Operation
ME: Monitor and evaluate ME4.5: risk management ME4.7: Independent assurance	Continual Service Operation

A.8 PCI/DSS

The PCI (Payment Card Industry) Security Standards Council (www.pcisecuritystandards.org) is an open global forum for the ongoing development, enhancement, storage, dissemination and implementation of security standards for account data protection. It publishes several standards and supporting documents that can be fount on their web site.

The Data Security Standard provides a set of requirements for enhancing payment account data security. With that it helps facilitate the wide adoption of consistent data security controls. Subjects covered are amongst others: Information Security Management, policies, procedures, network architecture, and software design.

Although the standard is aimed at financial account data protection, Information Security Management as it is written in this book is compliant with the requirements in PCI DSS. In fact ITIL Information Security Management supplements the requirements specified in the DSS.

A.9   Information Security Management and certification

Certification of Information Security Management is based on ISO/IEC 27001. In it, the requirements for the ISMS are given.

Benefits of independent certification of Information Security Management against ISO/IEC 27001 are:
- It demonstrates the independent assurance of your internal controls and meets corporate governance and business continuity requirements
- It independently verifies that your information risks are properly identified, assessed and managed
- It shows that information security processes, procedures and documentation are formalized
- It proves your senior management's commitment to the security of its information
- Furthermore, the regular assessment process helps you to continually monitor your performance and improve.

Certification takes place by a certification agency, accredited by a (globally) recognized accreditation body.

As stated earlier, the ISO/IEC 27001 ISMS focuses on information security, not on IT. To prepare for certification, the most important requirements that have to be implemented are:
- Perform risk assessments to be able to
- Produce a Statement of Applicability (SofA), which shows (based on ISO/IEC 27002) the controls that are in effect, what mechanism is used to determine the need for implementation or the reason for no inclusion
- Initiate a continuous improvement cycle for Information Security Management, including a regular management review
- Implement the required registrations.

Annex B: Cross-references for ISO/IEC 27002 and ITIL Information Security Management

The table below sketches the cross reference between ISO/IEC 27002 Code of Practice for Information Security Management and ITIL v3 Information Security Management. It is not always an exact mapping, but presents an indication of where a subject could fit best. Only the best fit is given. References apply to the full subject, unless stated otherwise.

The following abbreviations are used to indicate the specific ITILv3 volume:
- SS: Service Strategy
- SD: Service Design
- ST: Service Transition
- SO: Service Operation
- CSI: Continual Service Improvement

ISO 27002 reference number and subject	ITIL v3 Information Security Management
4. Security Risks	4.1.1. SS Risk Management and aligning with business risks
5. Information Security Policy	4.1.1. SS Security Strategy
6. Organization of Information Security 6.1.4 Authorization Process for information processing facilities 6.1.8 Independent Review of Information Security 6.2.3 External parties, addressing security in 3rd party agreements	5.3 Organization of Information Security Management 4.3.1 ST Change Management process 4.4. CSI 4.2.3 SD Supplier Management
7. Asset Management	4.3.2 ST Service Asset and Configuration Management
8. Human Resource Security 8.1.1 Roles and responsibilities 8.3.3 Removal of access rights	Largely not in scope 5.3 Organization of Information Security Management 7.4 Access control See text below this table
9. Physical and environmental security	Not in scope See text below this table
10. Communication and operations management 10.1.2 Change management 10.2 Third party service delivery management 10.3 System planning & acceptance 10.8 Exchange of information 10.9 Electronic commerce services 10.10 Monitoring	4.5 SO and 7.3 Communication and operations management 4.3.1 ST Change Management process 4.2.3 SD Supplier Management 4.2.2 SD Service Catalog management 4.2 SD Service Level management and Supplier management 4.2.2 SD Service Catalog management 4.4.3 CSI Service measurement
11 Access control	4.5.5 SO Access Management

ISO 27002 reference number and subject	ITIL v3 Information Security Management
12 Information Systems acquisition development and maintenance	4.2 Service Design
12.6 Technical Vulnerability management	4.4.1 CSI improvement process
13 Information Security Incident Management	4.5.3 SO Incident management
14 Business continuity management	4.2 SD IT Service continuity management
15 Compliance	4.4.2 CSI Service reporting

Table B.1: Cross reference of ISO27002 and ITIL V3

ITIL Information Security Management does not cover the following subjects:

Human Resource Security
This subject is hardly addressed in ITIL v3. When implementing Information Security Management, Human Resource Security is, however, of great importance. Common control issues, with the reference number to the Code of Practice include:
- 8.1 Pre-employment: screening; Terms and condition of employment (non-disclosure agreements)
- 8.2 During employment: awareness, education and training (see section 5.2)
- 8.3 Termination of employment: Termination responsibilities; Return of Assets; Removal of access rights.

Physical and environmental security
This subject is outside the scope of ITIL v3. Common controls that should be taken into account, with the reference number to the Code of Practice, include:
- 9.1 Secure Areas: Create a physical secure perimeter; physical entry control, security offices, rooms and facilities; protection against external treats; working in secure areas; public access, delivery and loading areas
- 9.2 Equipment security: sitting and protection; utilities; cabling; maintenance; security 'off premises'; secure disposal or reuse; removal and transport of property.

Annex C: Literature and links

ISO standards – see www.iso.org

ISO/IEC 27001:2005 Information technology – Security techniques – Information security management systems – Requirements

ISO/IEC 27002:2005 Information technology – Security techniques – Code of practice for information security management

ISO/IEC 27004 Information technology – Security techniques – Information security management – Measurement

ISO/IEC 27005:2008 Information technology – Security techniques – Information security risk management

ISO/IEC 13335-1:2004 Information technology – Security techniques – Management of information and communications technology security – Part 1: Concepts and models for information and communications technology security management

ISO/IEC 20000:2005 Information Technology – Service Management

ISO 7498-2:1989 Information processing systems – Open Systems Interconnection – Basic Reference Model – Part 2: Security Architecture

ISO/IEC 15408 Information technology – Security techniques – Evaluation criteria for IT security

Other documents

[CAZ] Cazemier, Jacques A.; Overbeek, Paul L.; Peters, Louk M. (2000). Security Management. The Stationery Office. ISBN 0-11-330014-X.

[COB] CobiT http://www.isaca.org

[COS] COSO http://www.coso.org

[DEM] Deming, WE "Out of the crisis", 1982" MIT CAES, Cambridge

[ISF] The standard of good practice – ISF – www.securityforum.org

[ITI] ITIL version 3 official website – www.itil-officialsite.com

[JER] Jericho Forum, www.opengroup.org/jericho

[MIT] Mitnick, K,D; William, S,; The Art of Deception. Controlling the Human Element of Security, 2002, John Wiley&Sons, ISBN 0471237124

[NOL] Nolan, Richard. "Managing the computer resource: a stage hypothesis"; July 1973. Communications of the ACM

[PVI] PvIB; "Functions and roles in information security"; March 2005; www.pvib.nl

[SAB] SABSA www.sabsa.org, www.sabsa-institute.com

[SAL] Saltzer, Jerome; Schroeder, Michael; "The Protection of Information in Computer Systems"; July 1974; Communications of the ACM 17, 7

[TOG] TOGAF Version 9 www.togaf.org

[WAL] Walton, M "The Deming Management Model." 1986 Perigee Books, NY

ITIL Books

Van Haren
P U B L I S H I N G

English
€39.95
excl tax

Foundations of ITIL®V3

Now updated to encompass all of the implications of the
V3 refresh of ITIL, the new V3 Foundations book looks at
Best Practices, focusing on the Lifecycle approach, and
covering the ITIL Service Lifecycle, processes and functions
for Service Strategy, Service Design, Service Operation,
Service Transition and Continual Service Improvement.

ISBN 978 90 8753 057 0 (english edition)

English
€39.95
excl tax

Foundations of IT Service Management
Based on ITIL®

The bestselling ITIL® V2 edition of this popular guide is
available as usual, with 13 language options to give you
the widest possible global perspective on this important
subject.

ISBN 978 90 77212 58 5 (english edition)

English
€11.95
excl tax

ITIL®V3:
A Pocket Guide

A concise summary for ITIL®V3, providing a quick
and portable reference tool to this leading set of best
practices for IT Service Management.

ISBN 978 90 8753 102 7 (english edition)

Information
Security

Information Security
based on ISO 27001/ISO 27002

Provides an overview of the 'two' international information security standards. A much-needed guide used globally.

ISBN 978 90 77212 70 7   (english edition)

Implementing Information Security
based on ISO 27001 / ISO 27002

A succint guide for those requiring a guide to implementation issues, providing an introduction, overview and background to both standrads.

ISBN 978 90 77212 78 3   (english edition)